Finding a new life walking The Camino de Santiago

written by

Matthew Govan

Dedicated to

My proud and loving father, Brian

Acknowledgements

First of all, I would like to thank you, for your interest in my book. I hope that you find it, as amusing and inspirational to read, as it has been for me to live all of these moments. I imagine, some might say, this could be a form of closure for me. But, I see it as a way of sharing my story and perhaps, one-day. You may also take that first difficult step and change your life or something you don't like too.

I would like to say a big, thank you to all of you, who I have mentioned within this book and also to those of you who I haven't. My new life would not be the same without you. In particular though, an extra special thank you, goes to all of my family, for being there for me, whenever I have needed you and for all your love and support. I love you and am very grateful to you all!!

Also, a special thank you goes to; Rachel and to the person I met briefly on a Metropolitan Line train one, Wednesday morning. For without you both, none of what has happened to me would be true!

No matter who you are, whether we are friends or not.

I am who I am because of everyone.

What is the Camino de Santiago?

At the beginning of 2016, I had never heard of it before and had no idea what or even where it was.

The 'Camino de Santiago,' is a series of walking routes or pilgrimages, which all end at the famous Cathedral in Santiago de Compostela. A credencial or a passbook is required to entitle you to a stamp and a cheap night's stay in any given number of albergues, hostels and pensions, along whichever route one is doing. It's also particularly important, if you would like to receive a certificate in Latin, from an office in Santiago de Compostela.

So far to date, I have walked

750 kilometres, of the Camino Frances, which was a journey starting at, St Jean Pied de Port in France and goes through 4 out of 15 of the Spanish regions before ending up in Santiago. My favourite one is, La Rioja, the view of all the vines is wonderful.

In Easter this year, I walked 150 kilometres of the Camino de Portuguese from Oporto in Portugal to Tui, in Spain.

In stages over a few weekends in the summer, I covered a distance of approximately 150 kilometres walking the Camino de Madrid. Starting at the Royal Palace in Opera, Madrid, over part of the Sierra de Guadarrama Mountains to Segovia.

The most important to me so far is the Camino Frances. Also known as the 'Way' or 'The Way of St James.' Traditionally, it is deemed to be the route his body was carried before being buried under the Cathedral of Santiago de Compostela. If you are Catholic and complete the challenging walk, it is believed that all of your sins are forgiven. Nowadays, people walk the route, for a variety of different reasons. I believe the most common are; wanting to change something in one's life; recovering from the loss of a loved one or being in search of something. Over 100,000 people complete the walk every year.

To make sure you are walking the right path, there are a series of scallop shell signposts or yellow arrows to follow. Eventually they all end up at the Cathedral of Santiago de Compostela. I have found it great fun looking out for them and making sure to walk the right way. Although sometimes, they are very difficult to see and in some places there aren't any at all.

There are a lot of stories behind the scallop shell. The lines represent the different routes from all over the world ending up in Santiago. Medieval pilgrims carried one to use as a cup for drinking water. But, also it is believed to go back as far as pre-Christian times and the Camino was a fertility pilgrimage, taken by a couple that needed help to have children. It is also seen as a symbol that one is walking or has walked a Camino.

If you are reading this because you are like I was over a year ago and want to know more about the Camino de Santiago or maybe deciding whether you walk. My advice to you is simply this:

Get up on your feet; go out the nearest door, take as few belongings as possible and DO IT! Then, from that moment on, you should only ever look backward, if you are going to take a photo of the awe-inspiring views that you will be able to see.

A few first encounter questions

After you have finished packing, all of the unnecessary things that you don't need to take and have remembered your credential book. It is important, to remember some standard practice questions useful for when meeting anyone for the first time.

1. What's your name?

2. Where have you walked from today?

3. How's your feet?

Then, if their answers are good enough and meet your first impression of them, in a positive way, continue the conversation. If not, apologise to them and say, 'that you need to push on because your friend is waiting for you in the next town.'

Wish them a Buen Camino and walk very quickly away from them!

Following on from these questions and after all of the other things like, 'Where are you from?' and 'What do you for a living?'

It may feel right to ask certain people the big question…

Why are you doing the Camino?

For me, it was quite simple, I thought that I wasn't happy with my life and I wanted to make some major changes. But I had no idea what, when or where.

Several years ago, I was on holiday in Turkey, relaxing by a swimming pool, when I spotted a girl sitting on her own. I thought she looked beautiful and I quite liked her and mentioned it to my best mate, who dared me to go and speak to her. I mustered some courage within me and went over to talk to her and surprisingly; we got on quite well and ended up spending the rest of our time there together.

After the holiday, we kept in touch as 'pen pal' style friends. One day, six months later, I drove to the Lake District to visit her and spent the entire night complaining about my life or at the time more lack of a good life. Having recently completed the Frances walk, she suggested that I go to walk the 'way' too. Thinking about this now. Rachel, my friend, I am so sorry that I was such a bore that night!

When I returned to London, I went back to work and to living the same negative existence. For a few days, I thought about the idea of going to walk, but I soon started working all the time again and forgot all about it. Until one day, out of the blue, I received a message from her asking, 'how I was and if I had thought any more about the walk or if I had even looked into it.'

But, due to work being such an over powering part of my life, I hadn´t and I didn't give it much thought afterwards either, I was well and truly sucked back into the routine of work and didn't have the time to think. I was living to work and that was all I did.

A few weeks later, I remembered the idea of walking the Camino. So, I asked a colleague if he had ever heard of it. He asked me, 'If I had watched the film?' Obviously I hadn't. Otherwise I wouldn't have asked and the same as before, I did nothing about it either.

The following Friday, my colleague asked me, 'if I had watched the film yet?' Unsurprisingly, my answer was of course, 'No, I haven't.'

I was stuck in a working, before living life first, mind-set and wasn't able to change it. Which, on reflection now, maybe I was stuck in that bubble and rut for way too long!

I bought the film during a lunch break later that day and watched it as soon as I got home, at around 2 a.m. I was exhausted the next day getting up for work after only 4 hours sleep. The thought of going was becoming more and more tempting, but the pull of work was like gravity keeping me firmly stuck to terra firma.

After watching the film, I decided to look into it some more, so I searched on the Internet, what the Camino is all about. I found out the history behind it; a variety of books available; plenty of videos to watch and a lot of guidebooks and different routes to choose from. I saw a book with a funny front cover and a brilliant title, downloaded it and found it a very inspirational book to read.

On a Wednesday morning, in July 2016, I was on a Metropolitan line train going to work; feeling exhausted and fed up. I was thinking about my life and wished that things could change and be a lot better than it was. At one of the stations along the way, a pregnant lady boarded the train and being a gentleman as always; I stood up to let her sit down. While I was standing there, holding tightly onto one of the handrails that sometimes feel very greasy. Suddenly, I heard something drop on the floor, I looked down and right there in front of me, was one of the Camino guidebooks that I had seen all those weeks ago on the Internet! Talk about a coincidence! Therefore, believing in fate and things happening for a reason, I took this as a sign that I should go.

I had a really rubbish day at work and it was possibly even, one of the worst that I'd ever had. So I thought, you know what;

'That's it, enough's enough; I'm off!'

The first thing the next day, I handed my notice in and decided to leave. Later that evening, I booked a train ticket to St Jean Pied de Port. Ironically it was leaving London on St James' day too, (25th July.) I planned on taking Rachel's advice and go to walk the 'Way of St James.' Reflecting on this now, I think this was another sign that going to walk the 'way,' was definitely meant to be and something that I should do!

Whoever you were that dropped that book, between you and Rachel. You both instigated the decision for me to leave and started the path of change for me. I am very grateful and indebted to you forever! If only, I had spoken to you and said thank you at the time.

Background

In terms of my family and childhood, growing up was no different to that of any other young boy in our 'neck of the woods.' I have an older brother, a younger sister, mum, a stepdad, stepbrother and stepsister. We lived in average, ordinary, nothing-special sized houses in quiet suburban and countryside'y type places.

Our family holidays were always good fun, our grandparents had a flat right by the beach in Fuengirola, and so we spent a lot of summers there. My brother and I would play 'Baywatch' on the beach, my sister would make sandcastles and my dad played his own version of our innocent game, he called it, 'Bum-watch.'

The game 'Baywatch' consisted of, one of us shouting, 'quick, there's someone drowning.' Picking up our inflatable dinghy and running down to the sea like a pair of lunatics, while burning our feet on the extremely hot sand. When we reached the sea, we'd dive in, with one of us holding on to the rope of the boat and then swim front crawl very fast pretending to rescue the person drowning. After running out of energy that'd be it. I have no idea now how many times that we did this before it got boring, but I think it was a lot!

My sister would just watch and laugh. She had her own game, which was a lot more relaxed. Whenever we were in the sea or a swimming pool, she would put her hands on our heads and say, 'one, two, three, let's go under water.' After that, she would push both my brother and I under the water and when we'd come up, she'd say, 'it's a joke.' I don't think she ever got bored playing that!

Once or twice, we went elsewhere and further afield on holiday; France; Malta; Miami; Disneyworld and The Epcot Centre. Although I was very young when we went to America, I have never forgotten what happened there.

My dad, brother and I, went out on a boat with a guy called, Chip to explore a great big lake. I had taken my favourite teddy bear with me, who was called, Montgomery Moose. While we were having fun cruising around, my brother snatched Monty from me and threw him out of the boat onto a tiny little island that we were going past. He thought it was very funny, but I didn't and I started to cry.

Chip took us over to the island and told me that it was safe for me to get out, and retrieve him. So I hopped out and grabbed it, but they thought that it would be funny to back off a bit in the boat and pretend to leave me there. I, of course, didn't find it very funny and cried again. So they came back, I hopped in and off we went. My brother took him from me and threw him out of the boat again. This time he was floating in the water, when all of a sudden a crocodile stuck its head up out of the water, took a great big bite and then swam off. So, it was bye bye to my beloved Monty, the bear. I was very unhappy! At least I was until I was given a massive ice cream.

As siblings, my brother, sister and I, never always saw eye to eye. My brother and I would fight sometimes and I would sing horrible rhymes to my sister. Now, I have always learnt from observing and listening to others, but what really made me learn to be quiet and peaceful, was seeing the fights that my brother and dad would have together. Ooff they were loud and some harsh words were said. I learnt from this to keep my head down and behave.

However, I wasn't shy of my own stroppy behaviour! At times I would get so upset, that I would take a bottle of pre-mixed Ribena and the biscuit tin and go outside to hide in my makeshift base, in the trees in the front garden. Only to be encouraged back inside by the two words, 'Dinners ready.'

Education

Growing up, I was lucky enough to go to two different private schools. The first was a lovely place in Middlesex. There was a school uniform to wear that consisted of a light green tie, grey shirt and trousers. In the summer we were allowed to wear grey shorts, with socks that had to be pulled up to the knees with light green garters to hold them up. The best part of the uniform though was the hat that we had to wear. Every time we saw a teacher we had to 'don the cap' and announce their name. It was great fun! I kept it for a long time until I went to a school disco party in Fulham, and some girl stole it from my head.

My favourite thing at that school was the swimming pool. There was a great teacher, who on Wednesday afternoons would be in charge of the snorkelling lessons. Trying to swim the entire length of the pool under water, without coming up for air was a lot of fun. Once I managed it three times and swam 75 metres, now though, after smoking for over 15 years, I can only manage 40-50 metres.

My second school was a boarding school. Here there was a uniform too, but sadly there was no hat to be 'donned' to the teachers. I had a special coloured tie, with the colours of the boarding house, that I was in instead. Every morning, I would get a coach from the train station and arrive at school for an 8:30 a.m. chapel service. I had lessons all day, some free time and dinner from 5:30 - 7 p.m. After dinner, I'd spend an hour and forty-five minutes doing my homework and then go home at 9 p.m. I didn't mind it, because it was good to get my work done. But, it was brilliant at the end of the day to escape and go home in my dad's shiny black monster of a car, A Mercedes E220.

The route that we used to go entailed going down a slip road that joins up with a motorway, which at night because there were no streetlights, it was the perfect place to let rip in his car. My word was it fast!! He would be tapping his fingers on the dashboard, listening to 'M People' or 'Frank Sinatra' while driving. I loved those journeys and still miss them even now!

Like any school experience, things weren't always rosy. One day, I was on my way back to my boarding house, when a boy from South Africa walked over to me carrying a very sharp looking pocket knife and said, 'Do you want to lose some weight, fat boy?' After a few seconds, of thought and slight fear, I grabbed hold of him, pulled him towards me, so that the knife was just touching my jacket and I said, 'Yes please, can you start here?' I don't think that it was quite the reaction that he was expecting. He asked me, to let go, but I didn't so, he ran away leaving the knife behind.

Another occasion was when I was sitting in my boarding house in the T.V room. The other boys in my year thought that it would be a good idea to bundle me and call me, 'Fat Matt,' then, punch me in the ribs and slap me around the head a few times. It was a regular thing for a week or so, until one day, I had enough of it and I stood up with such a force, growling like a grizzly bear, waving my arms around, trying to hit anything or anyone that was nearby. After that, they all just retreated out the door, and never did it again.

The worst of all was after school on the coach. I was going home early for six weeks, studying for my confirmation at our local church. Every night during the journeys home, a boy that was in the year below me was bullying me. He said things like, 'hello fat boy' and some other not very nice names. On the last night of going home early, the name-calling started up as usual, but this time there was a boy who didn't get the coach very often, who chirped up and said, 'Oh my god, are you going to take that.'

So I said to my tormentor, 'f*ck off.'

He responded by throwing a half full, 1-litre plastic bottle towards me. It hit my forehead with such force that it gave me a big fat bloody lump. I was then, encouraged by this non-regular, bus-riding boy to punch this bully over and over again. I was a bit like a raging bull until two other boys pulled me away from him.

My mum was in more shock than I was when she saw me at the station. My hands were dripping with blood and I had patches of blood all over my once, clean and white shirt. As soon as we arrived home, the phone rang and my housemaster had called, to find out what had happened. He said to my mum that the boy's injuries were quite severe and he had been taken to hospital with a concussion.

Going to school the next day was interesting, as there was a lot of staring, whispering and pointing at me. My housemaster called me into his study as soon as I arrived at school and he asked me what had happened. He explained, how some of the other boys on the bus had told him, that I had been bullied for the past month or so and how I was encouraged to attack him.

I was usually a quiet and a conscientious boy so, it was deemed out of character for me to have done this. But I still had to be punished for it. I was given was a Sunday night detention and had to clean the boarding house, do my homework and write 500 lines; 'talking about being bullied is far better than fighting.' It was a really easy punishment because after a few hours work, I was hiding in the television room, watching the omnibus of one of my favourite programmes.

To the person in question, if you read this, I am still to this day truly sorry for what happened. As for the person that encouraged me to react, I'd like to thank you for making me learn a lesson to never to be that person ever again!

I am not quite sure how, but I started working in the school kitchens on a Friday afternoon. I would make cakes for some elderly folk who would come and visit. Then I would help to cook the staff dinners. I found this much more fun than getting cold, wet and muddy. Oh, and not getting bruised from the nasty boys that would deliberately kick the ball at the 'fat boy' in goal. It was great fun and very satisfying, especially because I had a better excuse to escape from sports and activities. Rather than faking an illness and hiding in the warmth of the medical centre.

Turning point

All of a sudden, things changed forever! My dad had already been diagnosed with brain cancer. He had a benign tumour, which was treatable, so it was meant to be ok.

I was in the Library, which was the traditional type of place with the standard tall and dark wooden bookshelves. Slightly modernised in a sense that there was a separate computer room in the back corner. There I was, semi working, with one of the few sixth form only girls in the school. We were singing different songs playing on the radio. The song that we were singing at that exact moment was American Pie.

'A long, long time ago,
I can still remember how that music used to make me smile
And I knew if I had my chance
That I could make those people dance
But February made me shiver
With every paper, I'd deliver
Bad news on the doorstep
I couldn't take one more step
I can't remember if I cried
When I read about his widowed bride
But something touched me deep inside
The day the music died.'

I am not sure when it happened, during our singing of those words, that now seem very poignant having written them. But, there was a knock on the door and my housemaster was there. He was looking very sombre standing in the doorway and he said, 'Matthew, your auntie is here to collect you, your father is not very well.' So I gathered together my things and said 'goodbye' to my friend.

Walking outside the Library, I saw a very tearful auntie and a sad faced sister squashed in the back seats of her sporty, black Vauxhall Tigra. In my mind, I can still see the scenery and what that car was like. It is almost as if that whole situation is burnt onto a projector slide in my memory bank.

My auntie didn't say much, other than, 'your dad is in the hospital, your mum and brother are there and we are going too.'

According to my mum, he wasn't very well at home and she had to call an ambulance. When the paramedics looked him over, they said, that he needed to go to the hospital and gave him the option to walk or to be carried.

He walked.

When we left school, my auntie was driving a lot faster than I had ever seen her drive before and despite the circumstances was great fun. Vauxhall Tigras are fast little cars! Anyway, just under an hour later we arrived at the hospital, parked up and went in to see my uncle, mum and brother, who all looked very sad. My mum hugged and kissed us both through tearful, watery eyes and explained that it wasn't good news, but we were waiting on the doctors for some news. The clock, all of a sudden seemed to stop and the time passed so slowly just waiting.

My uncle, took me for a walk outside and I said to him, 'It is not good, is it?' To which he replied, 'No, I'm afraid not. It's time for you to be brave, strong and be there for your mother.' Which is something that I have always tried to be, although at the time it was very difficult. After our brief chat, we went back inside and the doctor was ready for us. We went into her office, it was a very plain looking room, neutrally coloured beige, possibly calming if you sat in there for a while, but for me, in that moment it felt constrictive and claustrophobic being in such a pokey space and even more so because she told us some extremely terrible news!

My father, a man who I had 18 years of getting to know, being loved by and returning love to, was soon to be no more. The tumour had grown and had burst a blood vessel. They had made him a bit more comfortable, but there was nothing else that they could do. We were told to say our goodbyes. My brother had already been in to see him, so I went in with my mum, but there was a big commotion and a panic, so we were kicked out and told to wait.

He had wet the bed. I felt a bit angry because it almost seemed like he had died in front of me there and then and I was unable to say goodbye. But no, not yet! He was fighting it good and hard. My second attempt at going in to see him was a lot more relaxed. Well, as much as it could be. When we went into the room, I saw a former version of what used to be my dad, with that trademark dark black comb-over hairstyle. There he was, with next to no hair, a vacant expression on his face and his skin looked very pale and cold. My mum said that she was going to leave me to spend some time with him.

At that moment, I felt really sad and extremely upset. I didn't know what to say, whether to move or what to do. So I just stood there on the spot for a minute or two. Then, I calmly took his hand and held it tightly, it felt different somehow, and was definitely not the same one that used to swing me in the air with my mum walking down the Fuengirola promenades. It was cold; it felt smaller somehow and then, I said some things that I have never and probably will never forget.

'Dad, I love you so very much and am going to miss you so much! I will do my best at school, in my A levels, at university and I will make you proud.' I think that I then said goodbye, gave him a big kiss on his forehead and left.

Shortly after we went home for tea and bed. I tried to sleep, but I'm not sure if I actually did. The next day, my mum asked if I wanted to go and see him again, but I just couldn't. I had said my goodbye and I couldn't handle it again. I wanted to remember the comb over and nice dad face, that I grew up seeing and not the empty, dying look. Unfortunately though, this hospital scene is also burnt onto a projector slide in my mind.

Later that evening, my mum and brother, returned from the hospital and said that he had died. 18th March 2000 at 18:45.

During his funeral, I read the poem, 'If' by Rudyard Kipling. Usually, reading out loud has never been that difficult for me, but this time it was different. I struggled at being able to read with a clear and loud voice. It was difficult trying to hold back the tears and stop my stomach from trembling so much. It was one of the most challenging five minutes of my life. Reading out loud with a heart that felt like it was beating far too fast and was going to burst out of my chest made it more of a horrible experience than it already was. I also remember seeing a lot of faces I did not recognise, all packed into one room! The relatively quiet church that we went to every Sunday and at Christmas was rammed. The door couldn't close for people's heads peeking around it. Which is a true testament to what an amazing man he was and someone I aspire to be and to make proud!

Celebrating my 18th birthday with my dad and family
The present was a 'This is your Life book.'

University

I went to university and studied a Hospitality Management degree, partly because I loved the experience of working in the school kitchens and also because I'm a sociable chap and wanted to work with and meet other people.

Being only 18 years old, away from home for the first time in my life and having just lost my dad, it was very hard. I found it so difficult that I decided to fly to Malaga and go to Fuengirola for a few days. It was an emotional trip and definitely wasn't the same as the family holidays that we used to have there. I went straight to, 'Manuel's' beach bar, who was very sad when I told him what had happened. He gave me a big plate of my favourite 'Boquerónes' for free and said, 'if I needed anything while I was there, to go and see him.' He was such a kind man!

To try and work through my grief, I had quite a lot of counselling sessions. During one session, I was asked, 'how I was?' I replied, that I was just plodding along as usual and they responded, 'No, you are not a plodder; you seem far too jolly for that. I would say, you are more of a bouncing along type of person.' I'm still not quite sure what this means, but I think it's a good thing?

Things for me seemed to be on the up. I was working as a waiter in a restaurant and made some new friends. After work one night, I even kissed a girl in a nightclub nearby too. It was certainly memorable because she had such bad breath!! It was almost as if she had eaten a whole bulb of garlic on its own for her dinner.

In my third year at university, it was time to get some practical hospitality experience, I went and worked at a sports and events stadium and had the time of my life. When I returned for my last year, I decided that it was time to work and make sure I passed. I studied more and was promoted to an assistant managers position with more money. I stopped drinking as much beer, saw a nurse to lose weight and lost 20 kilograms but best of all, I passed my degree!

Catering

A fantastic industry to be in for the buzz, pressure and sociability amongst guests and if you are in the right place even working amongst friends too. For me, it was a mixture of everything!

Working at the sports and events stadium during university was incredible. I was allowed to spend time in each department and gained a lot of experience. One day during the season, I arrived at work to be told by the Operations Manager, that I was going to be in charge of the corporate hospitality for the forthcoming test. Around 400 people were to have breakfast, lunch and afternoon tea. I would be given a staffing list, wine list, menus, etc. and be left alone to run it.

A famous cigarette brand was the sponsor that year. They were hosting the hospitality area I was looking after. Obviously not wanting to miss out on some free marketing, they had scattered around the room, in every place possible hundreds of these glistening gold packets of death sticks. They were everywhere!!

I was sucked in by temptation seeing all these packets, so somewhat shamefully; I snaffled quite a few of them into my bag. It was a nerve wrecking experience being only 21 years old and being seriously thrown in the deep end. I had to smoke quite a few cigarettes and drink lots of coffee before I had built up enough courage to brief the staff and get on with the day.

When all the service was done for the day the Senior Operations Manager came in and I was given a lot of praise for not; bailing out; cracking up under pressure and generally for not f**king it up. So I was allowed to do it again for the rest of that game and a few others too. The number of guests gradually became more and more too. It was such an amazing experience and is certainly one I will never forget.

After a while, I was asked if I wanted to experience something else. 'How did I feel about running the 18 bars around the ground and working as the Public Catering Manager?' I was taught how to clean the beer lines and 'tapping' up the beer barrels and gas bottles. I was also sent on a training course on, 'how to make the perfect sandwich.' Which it seems is a precise, almost art form, using a variety of sized ice cream scoops for each particular ingredient. The ingredients all had to be spread 'corner to corner.' When I returned to the stadium after the course, I was told to make, 1000 rounds of sandwiches for the next test match. Which was great fun, but using this technique for that many sandwiches was very time consuming and challenging to get them done on time.

I was even lucky enough to be responsible for the rebranding of the pricing tariffs and designed some conference paper. Some of which I still have, with some autographs on too. It was an amazing year out from university. The funniest occasion was during a quiet game when I had gone into one of the member's bars to snaffle a roast beef sandwich from a mate that was the chef who worked there. I was standing behind the bar with my tie off, about to get stuck in and eat the best bits of beef. When the door suddenly opened and a very well known comedian walked in and asked;

'Have you seen my wife?'

To which I replied, 'I'm sorry sir, but no.'
(I had no idea, what his wife even looked like.)

He replied;

'Good, well if it's not too much trouble. Can I have a pint and a whiskey then please?'

It was a hilarious moment and one that I will never forget. Not just because of who it was, but also because I had a big dollop of horseradish on my shirt, which I was trying to hide from him and was really hoping wasn't going to fall in his beer when I put it onto the bar for him.

During my time there, I was also able to go and work at five major horse racing stadiums, managing bars that had to be built from scratch using nothing but a table, ice buckets and a cash register. Each time, I managed to sell a ridiculous amount of alcohol and take a fortune in cash and occasionally when the card machines worked would make an obscene number of credit/debit card payments too. At one of the race meetings, the ice from some of the buckets leaked through the ceiling made a big mess and made me popular person.

My best memory that year was when I was asked to go and work at Buckingham Palace for a summer garden party. After clearing through very strict security. I was allowed in as a waiter wearing the shiniest shoes and cleanest, freshly washed and ironed clothes that I have ever worn. My job was to 'circulate' with a tray of drinks offering wine, orange juice or water to the guests. Which may sound like an easy task but, if you have clumsy hands and are sometimes nervous around lots of people, it's not! So, there I was 'circulating' and with an occasional tray wobble when suddenly, I heard some voices that sounded very familiar! In that particular moment, I felt honoured to be where I was standing, but my how it was scary! Seeing faces that I would only ever see in a newspaper or at Christmas on the television. I froze on the spot for what felt like ages and thought;

'Hmm, there are some extremely important people and I am standing here right next to them! Something's not quite right, then I looked down at my tray and thought about offering them a drink but noticed that I'd run out of orange juice and we were told to have all the drinks on offer on the tray.' So I retreated to the back of house area and felt very humble for a while.

After graduating from university, I was invited to return to work at the sports ground. However, I was given more responsibility and had the task of logistics thrown in the mix too. I had to move and shift a lot of furniture, set up all the bars, and then manage them during the match days. It was a very hectic job, but I loved it! During one particular week, I worked 96 hours and was almost a write-off for physical exhaustion the following week.

At the end of that season, the company I was working for asked me, 'If I wanted to go and work on a boat as an Events Manager?' I said, 'Yes.' It was very different, working on a boat rather than the stadium. Especially going up and down ladders all day and getting stock out from the wine cellar, which was a big room behind a massive bulk head and hatch. It was a brilliant place to be and I loved it. I gave tours to events guests around the ship, had my early morning coffee and smoke on the foredeck, while watching people cross over the bridges, almost like ants carrying food back to their nests.

One night, I even got talking to a very beautiful woman outside, under the moon and the stars. She had organised her companies Christmas party. Some of the guests were smoking inside the museum part of the ship, which caused the fire alarms to go off. The policy if this happened was to evacuate the ship. Despite my telling them not to, the alarm went off three times! Chasing 150 people and 20 staff off a boat, essentially on your own because of the less than agile and more overweight than me security guard, was extremely hard work! It was a fabulous job and is one of the best I've had so far.

However, after a few years and because I had saved some money, it was time to take up an offer presented to me by the Chief Executive at the sports ground;

'If you'd like to go to Australia one day, get in touch?'

So I did and I decided to go travelling. Although, having worked my socks off and developed an impressive C.V, I thought that it would be best to plan my trip around work. I didn't want a year away to cause a detrimental effect on my hard work record. I wrote to the Chief Executive, at the sports ground, who put me in touch with someone who worked at a similar stadium in Melbourne, Australia.

I managed to line up the prospect of some work there, but I also thought that it would be good to get some experience in America either, for before or after. So I booked an around the world ticket and went to see some family friends who lived in Los Angeles and shortened the long journey.

A family friend, Gary, picked me up at the airport and kindly took me under his wing and looked after me. He had organised some interviews for me at some hotels that his wife's family owns. He also arranged for me to go to a golf club in Palos Verdes, California. It was such a beautiful place that overlooks the coast. I stayed at their house and was very lucky to borrow his green Mini. My, what a great car that is, to drive along the California Coast! Although, driving on the opposite side of a car and road is very strange!

While I was there, they took me to Disneyland, San Diego and we went to see their boat too. Which was lovely and great fun to go on-board! The interview I had at the golf club was a great success and they offered me a position as a Restaurant Manager. Gary organised an attorney to help me to get a visa. While this was happening, I went to some other places further north for a few days.

My first stop was, San Francisco, which truly is a beautiful place. One day, I would love to go back and visit again. Seeing the trams, and 'Mrs Doubtfires' house was great to see. I went over on a boat to see Alcatraz too which was amazing to see, but it was quite eerie walking past all the old prison blocks with shattered glass windows. While I was there, I went to see a hotel, which was lovely to look around, but was nothing quite as special as the Los Angeles golf club. I hoped that my visa application would be approved and that I could work there!

Portland was my second stop and when I arrived, my first thought was, 'blimey, how many bookshops and barbers can there be in one town?' It's almost as if on every street corner, they would be there next to each other. I went and saw another hotel, which was incredible. I was met and showed around by the General Manager who was a very kind and charming man. He also offered me a job as a Restaurant Manager and allowed me to join him for lunch in the hotel dining room. Which, I think was possibly, one of the best lunches that I ate during my entire year away!

Seattle was my final stop, and I saw another hotel. The décor and building was beautiful, but everybody I met there, just seemed to have this, 'I'm a lot better than you, go away,' kind of attitude. So I didn't like it very much. Eventually, it was time to return to L.A and find out that unfortunately, I wasn't able to get a visa and couldn't accept either of the jobs. I didn't mind though because at least I was off to work in Australia!

I landed in Sydney around the time of my birthday and had a wonderful weekend there. I ate the best Eggs Benedict, Spinach, Bacon *(substituted the ham)* and Hollandaise sauce that I've ever had in a café in Darling harbour. I even met a nice girl in the hostel I was staying in and we went out on a date. We went for a walk around the harbour and the opera house then sat relaxing in the sun with a lovely milkshake.

Then, living up to my reputation of being clumsy, I managed to spill most of it down my front. I felt a bit like, the character, Albert in the film Hitch. Unfortunately, it also happened at the same time as a seagull decided to drop its guts on my shoulder. I was not impressed, but it made the girl I was on a date with laugh in hysterics. Even now, I have always been able to make people laugh, mostly because of my clumsiness, but also because I can be quite quick-witted and make the best out of a bad situation.

After cleaning up all the mess on my T-shirt, we went on the cable car that goes over and around the harbour, which was great fun. When it was time to get off, she stood up and had some chewing gum and a scrap of newspaper stuck to her shorts and her perfectly formed bottom. So, it was my turn to laugh a lot! What a right pair we made. I think that was possibly one of the best dates that I have ever been on. It was a lovely day with lots of laughs and she was just such a great girl! Unfortunately for me, she is now happily married. Something's just aren't meant to be sometimes. Although she is very happy, so I'm happy for her.

We all have our own 'lobsters' somewhere.

After a few more days there, it was time to earn some money and do some work. I said 'goodbye' to Sydney and went by bus and train down to Melbourne, where I managed to start working straight away. My first job was to drive a 'Ute' around the Formula 1 racing track in Yarra Park. I was delivering stock to the bars and occasionally picking up attractive hostesses and giving them lifts. Flirting and getting kisses from them was an incredible start to my Australian adventures. My English accent seemed to be a definite advantage. Being fat and overweight just didn't seem to matter.

Working at the stadium, there was a vastly different experience to the one in London. The place is enormous! I had a similar job to my previous one. I was responsible for over ten different outlets and bars. My job was to set them up for a match day, filling the fridges, putting things out on display, making sure all the stock, etc. was there for the bar supervisors. Then during the match days, I managed them, fetching extra items and helping out whenever it was needed. It was much harder work there, purely because of the distance between each of these places and the heat.

During one particular game, a bar that was the furthest away from the stock control base had run out of beer. I radioed my colleagues but didn't get any response. So I ran back to 'base' grabbed a pallet jack and a double-stacked pallet with 16 x 11kg kegs of beer on it. There were eight barrels per pallet, I then ran around the ground, pulling these pallets behind me to the bar at the very far end of the stand. Somehow with brute force and strength, I managed to do the magic three-point turn with the pallets in the lift, so that the pallet jack and I were ready to get out at level 1. I got the thing out and put every one of those barrels away in the cellar and was given a raucous round of applause and a cheer from a bar packed full of Aussie's who were previously raging because there was no beer for them to drink. I was dripping with sweat from the panicked hard work and the 40°c heat! Only then did my other colleagues turn up. 'Sorry Pommy, we were stuck elsewhere delivering some paper cups.' As you can imagine, at the time, I was not impressed!

It was the best experience being away from home for a year, travelling the west coast of America and everywhere in Australia except for Ayers rock and the north coast. Working at the stadium was bloody hard work but, brilliant fun. All the people I met were lovely, and I was very lucky that my hard work had paid off and I was offered a permanent job with a fantastic salary.

The company I worked for, was going to sponsor me to stay and had offered me a full-time job. It was really exciting and a great turn of events, after being unsuccessful with the jobs and visa in America. Unfortunately, the week before I was due to come home. One of the senior managers called me and said, 'that they were unable to sponsor me because they would be responsible for the cost of any medical injuries that might happen to me.' However, they said, 'that they would keep the job for me for a few months if I could get a visa on my own.' Sadly though, I had no luck with that, because I couldn't get enough points on the Australian skills list and had to turn down the job.

I returned to London in January 2007 and was offered a job as an Events Manager, working for a company based in South London. I was told to move closer to their offices, so I found a room to rent and moved in two days before starting work for them on a Monday. By Thursday of that first week, they called me into an office and said,

'I'm sorry, but we are going to let you go.'

Their reason was, 'You are not the right fit for our business because you are not aggressively dynamic enough and you shouldn't have asked the Managing Director to help you to tie your bowtie on your first night of working for us.'

(Firstly, I didn't know he was the MD, and secondly, I was standing in front of a mirror in the most disgusting staff room toilets that I have ever been in.)

They paid me some money in cash, there and then and said goodbye. What a great company to almost work for!

I felt very angry and let down by that company, for a long time, but now if I were ever to meet the person that said that to me. I'd like to thank them because I learnt a big lesson! Ironically, it is also something that I read about in a book called '101 ways of how not to treat people.' I think I saw it in the top 10 of the list too.

After that blow to my confidence and having rent to pay, I couldn't afford to waste time feeling sorry for myself. So, I had to get back out there quickly and get some money coming in to cover the bills. My first emergency option was the company that I worked for at the sports stadium. I was very lucky that they were kind enough to let back me in the door again and paid me a very good wage. They were able to give me enough work to help get me by until I found a permanent job as a Deputy General Manager. I was based in the head office of a prestigious charity. Within the very grand building, there was a member's only dining room, a lounge, a bar and a few rooms that were used for events and could cater up to 350 guests.

Such big events didn't happen very often. However, one that does stand out in my memory was saying hello to some of the cast from a magical film that had just come out in the cinema. They were very friendly and complimentary of my hard work. I felt very honoured to have once again been in the company of some great people, even if it was just for the briefest of moments.

It seemed like a great job for a while, until one day, I realised that my direct manager was an alcoholic and he liked one of those special refill cups with an ever-lasting drink in it, a bit like a gobstopper. But, it was one with an A.B.V. and a booze flavour, rather than the usual bubble-gum finish.

I didn't feel too worried though because, with the experience that I had gained in events until then, I was ok at surviving that part of the job. The rest of it though was not quite so easy. For example, managing my time to be in an office, ordering things needed for events, hiring and training staff, writing restaurant menu's and cashing up the takings. I was also paying salaries including my own, doing weekly accounts work and somehow managing to blag my way through financial conference calls with the Senior Management. I was working way over 65 hours a week and found it all extremely stressful and overwhelming.

In March 2008, I went on a training course with two of the ladies who worked in the sales office. We were going to learn about a new booking system. We stayed in a hotel nearby and had a great time together! The training was relatively interesting as far as I.T stuff goes. But the hotel, the food and the drinking were a lot more fun! We all got a bit drunk on our last night there and had a lot more laughs than we did at work in London.

The course was very interesting and it was nice to get away, but it was good to get back to familiar surroundings. That was at least until I walked through the door at work, to find out that I wasn't able to have the night off and that nothing had been done for the following week's events. The wages and the accounts for that week hadn't been done; the staff hadn't been confirmed for the Saturday wedding or the following week. The orders for Linen, Liquor and disposables also hadn't been placed! I was so fed up and was tempted to stick two fingers up and walk out. But, I have never been that unprofessional and I certainly would never actually do that, as much as it was tempting to do so at the time.

Turning point part 2

During that year, I was very lucky to be in a relationship with a beautiful Brazilian girl, who conveniently, was a waitress in the restaurant. When I got back to work from the Midlands, we were both delighted to see each other and spend some time together for a while before she had to work and set up the event that was taking place that night.

It was mid-afternoon and I was sat busily working away at my desk. When all of a sudden, I woke up and found myself lying on the floor suffering in a great deal of pain. Literally everything hurt all the way from my head down to my toes, even the insides of my mouth hurt too. I had no idea where, or who I was. I couldn't move or see anything, but I recognised a familiar voice. Which belonged to a kind and gentle giant of a Kosovan man, who was responsible for the health and safety and first aid within the building.

It took a long time for me to come around, but when I did, I realised that I had blood all over me and was very cold and sweaty. My trousers were very damp and I felt exhausted and was aching all over. When my eyesight became less blurry I saw two green outfits that looked just like big Jelly Babies. They were asking me if I knew what my name was, where I was and what day it was. Apparently, I was looking around at the walls, because I must have remembered that there was a large annual holidays calendar somewhere in the room.

The green suits were obviously paramedics, after asking all their questions; they looked me over and told me that I needed to go to a hospital. They asked me, if I wanted to walk or be carried out of the building. In that moment, I instantly thought of my dad and began to fear for my life, in case I had cancer too or if there was something else wrong with me, but I didn't know what. I was petrified!! So I opted to walk, which was a bad decision because it bloody hurt, but I just thought...

If my Dad can do it so can I.

My girlfriend at the time came with me in the ambulance and sat with while I had a blood test, an MRI scan and some X Rays and I was then eventually allowed to go home. My mum was away at the time, so my Auntie came to see me and took us both home.

The blood that was all over my white shirt was caused by sharp contractions of my teeth, biting away at my tongue and removing over ¾ of it. I was signed off work for a few weeks and spent most of that time in bed. I was knackered and still in a lot of pain. Also because of my tongue or lack of, I could barely speak or eat! In a way, it was great though, because I lost so much weight! If only it would be so easy now. However, the tongue is one of the fastest healing organs in our bodies, so it didn't take long before I could get stuck in and eat some hearty 'Mummy Govan' cooked dinners and put all the weight back on again.

I was taken to see a Neurologist in a London hospital. He was a very kind man, who reassured me that I was going to be fine and that they had found nothing sinister from any of the tests, which put me at ease a lot. I was referred for some further examination at the National Epilepsy Hospital in Stanmore. Which is a place that I really don't like to visit. Like any other disease it is hard to endure, but I think that Epilepsy is a particularly sad disease to be suffering from. Seeing people walking around wearing crash helmets made me feel scared s**tless and I hoped that I wasn't going to need one and have to stay there.

There was a test I had, where I was sitting in a telephone box style room, with disco lights and flashing camera effects going off in my face. While I was in this box, I prayed to God and spoke to my Dad. I asked them both and wished that everything would be ok and that it wouldn't happen to me again. The results of the tests came back as inconclusive and it was deemed that the seizure was a one-off, but I needed to take better care of myself. I was told to eat properly, work and smoke less and get more sleep. Oh, and also drink a lot less than 20 cups of coffee a day!

Returning to work

It was not easy going back to work after this, especially with everybody in the building knowing about it. I felt somewhat of a special case. I was told to be on light duties for a while and limited hours, which was fine for around two weeks until the GM was back to his routine of drinking a lot and me working too much! Which unfortunately resulted in me having a second seizure.

I was at home one day and I'd had a lovely evening with my ex-girlfriend and we had gone to bed together as normal. However, when I woke up, I was in a hospital and I had no idea, how I got there or for how long. It was frightening, especially because it had happened twice.

Fortunately, it wasn't as bad as the first seizure and my tongue was still in tact. I stayed in the hospital for a few hours, had the same tests done and was eventually allowed to go home. I was incredibly hungry, so we went straight to Sainsbury's. My ex; was holding me up the whole time as I hopped around buying most of the food the shop because I couldn't make up my mind what I wanted. In the end, when we got home, I fell asleep straight away and didn't get to eat any of the delicious dinner that was cooked for me.

I went to see a Neurologist again and was given the same answers. There were no underlying causes or any explanation as to why the fits were happening. He prescribed me some medicine to take twice a day, to see if it prevented any more fits from happening. He also explained that the risk of further seizures drops exponentially every year that passes. The medicine did the trick for a few years, until one day, when I was very silly and decided that I didn't need to take it anymore. I had moved house and the doctor's surgery I was registered with, wouldn't supply the medicine to me any more, because I wasn't living in their borough. I had picked up a form for a new surgery, completed it but didn't return it and register. What a bad mistake that was!! I went to bed at home and woke up in a hospital after having yet another fit! Now knowing it clearly works, I am never going to stop taking it!

Camino de Santiago Frances

I had misread the time that I was meant to leave and was almost too late to get on the Eurostar at Kings Cross Station. After saying a rushed goodbye, I just managed to board and find my seat in time before it left. In hindsight, I am pleased that it was a quick goodbye because I cried my little heart out walking away from them at the ticket barriers. I had very mixed emotions of both excitement and fear.

I had a week in St Jean de Luz to relax on the beach first. But I ended up suffering in pain for most of the time because I have arthritis my right hip and knee. I have had steroids injected into my hip twice and the last time I had it done, the doctors told me that one day, I would need a hip replacement. But they said that I was young to have it done now. Unfortunately, the steroids didn't seem to work during my time there, so it wasn't quite the holiday that I was hoping for. It scared me a lot, especially when I was thinking about the very long walk that I was about to do. I must be mad I thought!

Despite my fears, I decided that I hadn't gone all that way for nothing. I built up the courage and went to St Jean Pied de Port. I had rented a room in a house with a lovely American lady. She picked me up at the train station, took me to the office where I got my first stamp in my credential book. We had the usual get to know you chat and she asked me what was wrong with my leg because she had noticed that I was walking funny. I explained the story behind the pain in my hip and said that I was considering not doing the Camino. The whole time I was thinking negatively, 'I can't walk over the Pyrenees!' She said I would be fine, but also that there is an alternative Camino trail for the less abled, that isn't as bad as the main route. The next day, she took me for a drive to the end of the day one place, Roncesvalles. She drove on the road that runs parallel to the pathway. After seeing what it was like and spending that night being reassured by some nice French girls.

I made up my mind; 'I can do it and I will make my dad proud!'

My walking route: from; 2nd August until 5th September 2016

Day 1 – St Jean Pied de Port to Roncesvalles: 27k
Day 2 – Roncesvalles to Zubiri: 24k
Day 3 – Zubiri to Pamplona: 22k
Day 4 – Day off for some R&R
Day 5 – Pamplona to Puente la Reina: 26k
Day 6 – Puente la Reina to Estella: 24k
Day 7 – Estella to Torres del Río: 30k
Day 8 – Torres del Río to Logroño: 21k
Day 9 – Day off because of a major hangover
Day 10 – Logroño to Nájera: 31k
Day 11 – Nájera to Santa Domingo de la Calzada: 22k
Day 12 – Santa Domingo to Belorado: 24k
Day 13 – Belorado to San Juan de Ortega: 25k
Day 14 – San Juan de Ortega to Burgos: 27k
Day 15 – Day off because of yet another hangover and tendinitis
Day 16 – Burgos to Castrojeriz by bus
Day 17 – Castrojeriz to Frómista: 26k
Day 18 – Frómista to Carrión de los Condes: 28k
Day 19 – Carrión de los Condes to Terradillos: 28k
Day 20 – Terradillos to Sahagún: 13k
Day 21 – Sahagún to El Burgo Ranero: 18k
Day 22 – El Burgo Ranero to Mansilla de las Mulas: 20k
Day 23 – Mansilla de las Mulas to León: 20k
Day 24 – León to Hospital de Órbigo: 34k
Day 25 – Hospital de Órbigo to El Ganso: 32k
Day 26 – El Ganso to El Acebo: 25k
Day 27 – El Acebo to Villafranca del Bierzo: 40k
Day 28 – Villafranca del Bierzo to La Faba: 25k
Day 29 – La Faba to Triacastela: 25k
Day 30 – Triacastela to Sarria: 26k
Day 31 – Sarria to Portomarín: 24k
Day 32 – Portomarín to Eirexe: 18k
Day 33 – Eirexe to Melide: 23k
Day 34 – Melide to O Pedrouzo: 34k
Day 35 – O Pedrouzo to Santiago de Compostela: 20k

Daily Routine

Before I go into the miracles and explain what happened to me during my adventure. I want to outline some daily things that have been the same on all of my Camino's so far and could be for your too if you walk or have already walked one.

Be prepared for a lot of the same things! For example, to be woken up at 5 a.m. to the wonderful sounds of zips, going up and down, banging, crashing, teeth brushing and toilet flushing. Occasionally, there may also be mattresses squeaking and people falling out of the top bunk and landing with a loud thump. (Not that that happened to me of course.)

Leaving places at around 6:30 a.m., to fulfil the same goal as the day before, getting dressed, packing up your things and walking out through a different door every day.

Then putting one foot in front of the other for, between 6-8 hours, until you end up at the end goal place for the day. Sometimes also hoping that by putting one leg first that the other one will actually follow. In regards to feet, be careful of sprained ankles and be prepared for blisters.

Drinking, lots of café con leche, iced tea, and gallons of water. Eating toast with tomatoes, olive oil and salt for breakfast or a Spanish tortilla bocadillo, in fact at any given rest stop to eat any type of bocadillo. Depending upon the time of year, your size and physical ability, sweating a lot. When arriving at an end goal destination, drink lots of wine, having some average dinners and sometimes an even more average nights sleep.

Some of the bedrooms may also be too hot, smelly, and you might have to listen to people talking in their sleep, farting loudly, snoring and fidgeting. Oh, and if you are lucky, you won't be woken up by someone having some right-handed fun on their own.

Day 1 – St Jean Pied de Port to Roncesvalles

Some might say that being scared of taking on a challenge is good for you, but I didn't quite see it like that! I was petrified. Despite my confidence the day before, I was thinking, 'could I really do this?' 780 kilometres is no short distance. Particularly, when I have always been fat, smoked too much and never really done much exercise. Not to mention suffering from epilepsy and arthritis. What if I were to be on my own and have a fit, what if my hip were to hurt so much that I couldn't carry on and nobody being around to help me! Too many 'what ifs.'

So, having said goodbye to the lovely American lady and the French girls who were walking the main route. I set off looking for the trademark yellow arrows. Things were going well until all of a sudden when I found myself back in the town of St Jean after walking around in a circle for just under an hour. My hip was starting to hurt and I started to feel fed up, scared and thought about staying there and not going anymore. But, something in my head said; 'No Matthew, for once in your life, don't be a failure and give up, you can do it, make your Dad proud like you promised.' So I took three ibuprofen tablets, said a prayer to the big man upstairs and off I went. Camino walking, take 2.

Walking on your own can be a therapeutic and peaceful experience, listening to the sounds of the birds, running water streams and the general outdoor, and the usual countryside noises. I occasionally listened to music to keep motivated. The first part of the walk was pretty easy. I stopped in a place called Valcarlos for lunch and ate some nice big chunks of cheese, chorizo and some bread and the biggest bottle of nice cold water.

While I was sat there on a bench, a man came over. He sat next to me and we chatted for a bit about the Camino until he left and wished me a Buen Camino. A few minutes later an elderly lady came over and asked me, 'What are you doing?' To which I replied, 'I am walking the Camino.' She was very shocked by this answer. She then asked, 'you are doing it on your own, do you not have any friends?' I was a bit taken aback by this and have often thought about it since. She then told me that she wanted to walk it with her parents, but her father had, had an affair and he had moved to America. Now, she hates America and doesn't want to know anything about the Camino. To which, I had no idea what to say. Fortunately though, she then just said 'goodbye' and walked off.

The next few hours from there on were slightly less eventful, apart from dropping my sweaty hat and having to walk back on myself for over half an hour to retrieve it. Unfortunately, this happened twice too. The walk became a bit nicer too because I wasn't on the main road anymore and the path was going through a forest. It was also starting to be very hot! I have no idea what the temperature was, but I imagine it was at least 30°c if not more. The more the weather got hotter, the harder it became to walk up the steep and rocky pathway.

I started to think about all the different bits of advice my family had given me.

Mum and Step Dad – Take it steady and drink lots of water.
Sister – Take lots of photos.
Brother – If you have a 'bunk up,' wear a condom.
Uncle – Remember you are there to see the sights not the floor, so remember to look up!

I thought about my Mum's advice first, which seemed sensible. I had the water and I was trying to take it steady. My sisters was next, I had already taken a lot of photos, even if they were mostly all the same. Grey tarmac roads, green trees and the occasional yellow arrow photos. My brothers, not much chance of a 'bunk up' happening here, especially when I had been on my own and hadn't seen anyone for at least three or four hours! My uncle's advice was last. 'Hmmm,' I was thinking, 'yeah alright, look up at what an endless steep path and a continuous heat wave?'

My thought's then turned to my advice to myself, 'F**K this.. It's bloody hard work and I don't like this feeling of sweating like I'm wearing a winter outfit and sitting in a sauna.' At which point, I threw my bag on the floor, sulked for a while out of exhaustion and loneliness, at not having anyone to talk to other than myself. I smoked a few cigarettes, drank a lot of water and ate a banana which all seemed to cheer up a bit. I also thought, 'come on Matthew; you are not going to get there just by thinking about it.' Although, that would have been amazing if such a thing were even possible.

I stood up and carried on until I realised that I had no idea where I was or how far away the next water fountain was meant to be. I had run out of water and was failing part 2 of my mum's advice. It must have been at least an hour or more that I was walking up through a very peaceful forest, feeling extremely hot and thirsty. I came out into a clearing and saw a house and thought YES: finally, there is somewhere to get some water!

No matter how hard I knocked, on the front door, nobody answered. Starting to fear of dehydration, I turned round with no option but to soldier on, but there right in front of me was the water fountain that I was searching for! I have never been quite so relieved in my entire life to drink some water! I ran straight over to the fountain and drank so much. I threw my boots off, chucked my bag on the floor and sat there for over an hour. Some guys from Cuba pulled up in their van, we chatted for a bit and they wished me a Buen Camino and drove off. It was a magical moment that gave me an extra boost to carry on.

The rest of the walk from there onwards was tough as the path was endlessly going up the mountain. Eventually, when I got to Roncesvalles, I had a very satisfied feeling, after around 7 hours of walking I'd finally made it! I was so tired but relieved that I had survived and arrived! I got a bed for the night and met some random German guy, who had such disgusting feet. He was popping his blisters and picking a lot of dead skin off right in front of me, while I was trying to write some notes in my diary. It made me feel sick and it still does at the thought of seeing them!

Still, that's by the by, we had a beer together and we went to the pilgrims mass in the church. I didn't understand a word of it until the blessing we were given by the priest at the end, who it turned out was Irish. While I was having dinner, there was a girl staring at me with a very strange expression on her face. At first, I thought that I had spilt food down my front, or that I had something wrong with my hair or face. I couldn't cope with it because I was knackered, couldn't wait to lie down and take my shoes off, so I ate quickly and went to bed.

The beautiful Pyrenees Mountains & the house of no water.

Day's 2 - 4 – Roncesvalles to Pamplona

I woke up the next morning at around 5 a.m. to the sound of zips, mattress springs squeaking, doors creaking, banging crashing, snoring, farting, coughing and the general noise of people movement. I was still exhausted and I had only walked for one day. I noticed a family who it seemed had woken up that early just to unpack their bags, re-fold everything and pack it again? I didn't understand why they were doing this, but it was very annoying because they were so loud!

In the end, I got out of bed and joined in with the noise brigade and decided to get going too. I packed up and shipped out, down to the same restaurant place as the night before. I ate a rather basic breakfast that consisted of underdone toast; some lukewarm coffee and orange juice which way too many bits in it. The whole time I sat there, the same scary smiling and staring girl was there freaking me out again. I worked out that perhaps it was because she 'liked' me. Heaven knows why I was lumpy around the edges and probably looked shattered and sunburnt! Eventually, I'd had enough of it again and it was time to get away and quickly. I saw a lovely looking Italian girl who was out the front getting ready to go and I was wondering how I could strike up a conversation and walk with her and her friends.

Unfortunately though, they had left. So, while I was getting myself ready to go, bag on, water bottle filled, picking up my walking sticks. I dropped one of them, and randomly decided to swear in Romanian, a word that I had learnt from a work colleague in London. Unfortunately, it was also one that the scary smiler knew and made her laugh a lot! She came over to me, introduced herself and that was it, despite being apprehensive about her, we became friends and left together.

The more we walked, I still couldn't forget about the strange smiling, but I wasn't brave enough to bring it up and ask. So we just walked and chatted about all the normal, boring things like, where are you from and what do you do, etc.

We were as thick as thieves for a few days. I didn't need to ask about the scary smiling, as I found out the answer, it was because she was interested and romance blossomed, which was definitely not something I went away from home looking for. However, it happened and it was great too. I didn't feel alone anymore and was happy to be having fun and having someone to walk with. Not to mention, that I also felt relieved that if something were to happen to me, that there was someone around to help. It felt like we were together for ages. Looking back at it now, I cannot believe that it was only two days as it felt like it was much longer.

Zubiri was the end of day two stop and my, what a lovely place it is! I spotted a swimming pool coming down from the mountain. Walking into the town, I knew that I was going to be able to swim there! Or at least I hoped because it was bloody hot! We found a place to stay and were very lucky because we managed to get the last two beds available. After getting settled and changed, we went looking for the pool, found it and were allowed in. It felt amazing, going for a very refreshing swim in a cold-water pool!

Afterwards, we went for a drink and met around 15 people of different nationalities. It turned out to be a big drinking fiesta and somehow the mixture of languages seemed to be understood by all. It was very amusing and was a really good night. I thought to myself, this Camino lark is not that difficult, it's only a very long walk.

The next day, we left for Pamplona after a late start, because I'd lost the key for the locker, where I had stashed my passport. The owner had to break into it for me. I lied and said, 'that the key had been stolen.' Although, I have no idea what happened to it, as it was in the pocket of my shorts? I have my suspicions that it might have fallen out when I was swimming. I was feeling very hung-over walking away from there, which along with hearing the noise brigade is something that I got used to quite quickly.

When I arrived in Pamplona, I thought, that it wasn't quite what I expected because it's a lot bigger and flatter than I thought it would be. I stayed an extra day so that I could send some really unnecessary stuff home. I don't know, why on earth I decided to take waterproof trousers, a camping groundsheet and my Kindle. I also sent the big and heavy hiking boots I was wearing. For some reason, they had become too small for my feet and were very uncomfortable!

'Your feet will swell in the heat.' Is what it said in that funny front cover book that I'd read. When I saw that I thought, that it couldn't be true. But, I should have believed it though because it is! I bought a new pair in a department store because it was the only place I could find some in my size. I had some help from a sales assistant who recommended them and 90€ later I was ready to go.

Day 5 – Pamplona to Puente La Reina

It was a very long, hot and tiring day. We left the hotel a bit late again, having had a good breakfast. For most of the walk, my friend and I were both very quiet. There seemed to be a bit of a tense atmosphere all day. I wasn't in the mood for a chit-chat anyway because I was getting used to being back out on the road again. Especially after being so lazy having a rest after only four days of walking.

We got to Puente La Reina at around 6 p.m., which is quite a late time to arrive. I was semi sort of worried about finding a place to stay, but what I was more concerned about, was where the nearest bar was so that I could have a nice and cold end of day glass of wine! Which as it turned out to be two or three bottles between us. We ate some tapas and had an awkward chat with two rather unfriendly French women who it seemed like were following me because they were always nearby.

It all went a bit down-hill after that as my 'friend' said, that 'she was going to leave me to go off and walk with another guy.' She apologised, for not being very talkative throughout the day and said, 'that she had been thinking about it all day.' It came as a bit of an unexpected shock really and I felt a bit gutted. Before I could get a chance to say anything, the guy in question arrived. It was almost as if she had thrown a carrier pigeon, delivering him a message to come along.

Feeling a bit uncomfortable, I left to try and find a place to stay, I was upset and a little pickled, from drinking too much wine. Fortunately, I found a place that seemed quite nice. I had a cold shower, which sobered me up a bit, but I still passed out as soon as I got into bed, watching the ceiling spin around.

Day 6 – Puente la Reina to Estella

When I woke up, I realised that I was the first up and managed to beat the bed bangers and bag zipperer's, by leaving first for a change. I was desperate to get out of the place and get a head start on my now ex-best friend and escape the feeling of sadness. It was not one of my best days and is a shame that such a beautiful place has been tarnished with a bad memory because Puente la Reina is a place worth a visiting!

I left at 5 a.m., in the dark and was feeling as adamant as I was about leaving London, to get out of there and fast. I felt awful and was really upset. I also now, never want to feel like that again!

A few years ago, my uncle gave me a wind-up head torch that was very useful on the one or two occasions I used it at home. However, during this particular morning, I think it was past its use by date and it just didn't want to work. The light would shine for around five minutes and then it would die out. I tried to give it 200 turns away from me and then a further 200 towards me. (Fast and slow charges, is what I remembered from the instructions).

I continued to walk, while doing this with a very loud;

Whiiirrrrrrrrrrrrrwhiiiiiirrrrrrrrrrrrrrwhiiiiiiiirrrrrrr noise

It was incredibly annoying too. Both my head and heart felt bad enough as it was, without adding to the pain that I was suffering from. I was walking on a white sandy type pathway while doing this and could kind of make out where I was going because all the stars were still out and the moon was shining very brightly. So, eventually, I gave up with the infernal noise machine and made do without it.

Suddenly I realised I needed the toilet, and the next one was a long way away. Fortunately, the guidebook I'd read said, 'pack a toilet roll, minus the cardboard inner to save weight and take some disposable bags in case of emergency, but remember to bag up your waste.' So, I did what needed to be done, bagged up the mess and packed it in an outside pocket in my bag. At that moment, it also felt like the kind of place to reflect on things.

I sat down, lit a cigarette and noticed that there was a disco going on in Puerta la Reina. I had noticed it earlier when I was filling my water bottle, but what with the torch and toilet drama; I hadn't thought about it. The song, the beat and the lyrics that was playing there and then was amazing and is a situation that I will never forget and not just because of the toilet stop either!

I live my day as if it was the last
Live my day as if there was no past
Doin' it all night, all summer
Doin' it the way I wanna

Yeah I'mma dance my heart out 'til the dawn
But I won't be done when morning comes
Doin' it all night, all summer
Gonna spend it like no other

It was a crush
But I couldn't, couldn't get enough
It was a rush
But I gave it up

At the time, I was felt terrible because of this particular girl; I started to think about all my other relationships, which have all been amazing, but very sad at the end. One of them even ended very badly because the girl in question was a tad violent. This short spell felt very different. It was only a three or four-day romance, but it felt like it was a much longer relationship. It was very strange. The lyrics of the song seemed to just go on and on, a bit like the 400 whirring noises. For some reason though, listening to it made me feel better somehow and it still does when I listen to it.

Walking onwards, both my head and my heart started to feel better. Suddenly though, I saw that there was a split in the road and no trademark yellow arrows anywhere to be seen in the dark. I looked around and suddenly remembered, that I had a torch on my phone. It still didn't help to find any arrows, but what I saw instead came out from the trees somewhere. A small bird came and landed pretty much right next to my foot and sat there for a few seconds. I noticed it and my shoelace being undone and then watched it fly/hop down the left-hand path. Taking that as a sign, I followed it and sure enough 10 minutes or so a bit further on there was a yellow arrow.

I felt very lonely there and I wished that I had some friends either walking with me or at home. I thought that, if only I hadn't worked so much and wasted so much money on cigarettes, that maybe my life would have been different. But, I was trying to be realistic and live in the moment, so I changed my thoughts to something else; 'Boy do I feel hung-over, yet again!'

A few minutes later, something else very strange happened! Just in front of me, there was a big bright light that had appeared out of nowhere. I carried on walking towards it, wondering what it might be, but when I got there, there was nothing and nobody to be seen and no one responded to my shouting either!

I still cannot explain, what it was or, where it came from, but I walked on continuing to think negative thoughts about being lonely, alone, lonesome, whatever you want to call it and also how I had worked too much. But then I stopped thinking about it and thought that perhaps that light in the trees meant something, but I didn't know what. The more I thought about it, the more this calming, tranquil sort of feeling came over me. I decided to turn around to see how far I had walked away from the town because I could still hear the disco music and was surprised because I had been walking for at least 2 or 3 hours.

When suddenly, something else very strange happened. Two guys just appeared, out of nowhere! I have no idea where they came from. They looked like father and son, but when they were next to me, the older chap just marched past very quickly and the younger guy decided to stop, talk and walk with me. We got on really well and chatted for the next few hours, we even stopped for a coffee in the next town and then lunch somewhere else after that. Eventually, he decided that he was going to walk on faster; he wished me a Buen Camino and very soon had vanished again.

After he left, I reflected upon how before the bird, the song and the random light I had felt lonely, sad and upset, then meeting him for a while, I realised that being lonely sometimes really isn't that bad. I experienced some magical things, which would have been nice to share with someone, but it seems, more special that it was just me that saw them and felt the emotions from seeing them on my own.

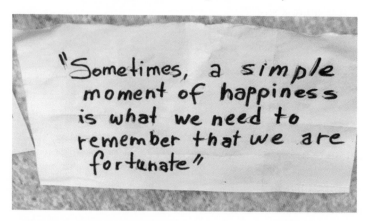

"Sometimes, a simple moment of happiness is what we need to remember that we are fortunate"

Days 7 - 10 – Estella to Nájera

I had a lot of mixed emotions and feelings that day and was very pleased when I eventually arrived in Estella. I met a couple from Finland and a guy called Mick, from Canada. The four of us became instant friends, which was lovely! Talk about a complete change of circumstances, from that morning's drama. We shared a few bottles of wine and some food from the only place that was open on a Sunday (the petrol station).

Later that evening we met a bunch of Italians. One of which, I think was the beautiful girl that I had seen and wanted to walk with on day 2. Laura her name was. She was getting all her friends to do their stretches, while shouting at them from the comfort of her perch on the bench next to me. It was very amusing to watch. Sadly they weren't around in the morning. So, she was just another girl that I'd met, liked and never saw again.

During that day, I walked with and overtook Mick and the Fins quite a few times. It seems I have quick little legs when I want them to be. We stayed that night in Torres del Río and had another nice evening together. We all had a very comfortable single bed and were able to go for a swim in a nice pool, although it was bloody freezing. It was a nice place to visit and is somewhere that I would consider going back to one day. It is quite a small village, with very old buildings, perched on a steep hill with wonderful views.

The four of us all walked to Logroño, which was lovely. We all got on really well. After finding a place to stay, we had some drinks in the square and then Mick and I went off on a bit of a bar crawl. It was only 1€ for a glass of wine. I think I only spent 20€ that night and was so drunk and full after eating a lot of delicious tapas from places along a street that is packed full of bars selling all sorts of different food.

Mick and I decided to stay an extra day in Logroño because it had such a good vibe to it. Also because the blisters on my feet were appalling and my two bad choices in footwear were starting to take their toll on my feet. Never do a long distance walk, wearing big heavy boots or branded trainers, bought by recommendation from a guy that works in a department store. I was walking in those shoes somehow with my foot tilted to the right the whole time, so I was almost walking on the sides rather than soles of my feet.

Day 10 – Logroño to Nájera

Mick and I had a walked together and had a very long 32-kilometre walk, in very hot weather. We arrived in Nájera, late in the afternoon, checked in to a beautiful little albergue next to the river. I was lucky again because I managed to get one of the last beds too. I had an amazing shower, as the water was hot for a change and washed my clothes in their washing machine for 5€. Which seemed very cheap. It was a great place to stay.

The albergue, had a lovely hand carved wooden dining table in the kitchen area and a bench, outside the front door that overlooks the river. It was a great spot to sit in the sun, write my journal and drink a cold and refreshing iced coffee.

When Mick was ready, we went off exploring the town, mainly in search of a bar and Camino juice (wine.) But first, I wanted to find a shoe shop because I couldn't carry on with the ridiculous pair I was wearing. I was very lucky and managed to buy a new pair, which seemed very comfortable and the best choice so far. Throwing away money is not something that I like to do very often, but putting those awful shoes in the bin was very satisfying! We then had success again and found a very cheap restaurant, ate some delicious Manchego cheese, Paella and some Patatas Brava's. There was a difficult decision to make while we were there though.

"What shall we drink today, white or red?"

Day 11 – Nájera to Santa Domingo de la Calzada

I had a great nights sleep that night, because the bed was extremely comfortable and the one bottle of wine I had to drink, was just enough to help me nod off and not have a spinning class when I got into it. The walk that day was very easy, mainly because we stopped for drinks stops a lot. Every day, we made a plan of where we were going to, as it was important to have a target to aim for. But it was more important to plan the day around food and drinks stops. Especially when the weather was getting hotter.

When Mick and I arrived in Santa Domingo, we met two nice Irish girls, Jane & Orla. It was a bit awkward how we met though. While we were in the Albergue bedroom getting settled in, Jane came in and had just got out the shower and was trying to get dressed. But, she couldn't because I was too busy talking to her. I couldn't remember her name though, so I had to sign language to Mick to introduce himself and find out. Which made the situation even more challenging for her, as the two of us were both going 'blah, blah blah' to her. Shortly afterwards, we met Orla in a bit more of the normal way.

Santa Domingo is a lovely place and also worth revisiting. There was a children's music concert going on which was incredible to see. Some of the fancy outfits that the people were wearing looked lovely and hearing them sing in the local church was amazing.

Day 12 – Santa Domingo de la Calzada to Belorado

Even though the music was great to listen to, I had a terrible nights sleep in Santa Domingo. The Spanish really know how to part! The music concert went on for hours. In the bedroom, there was a snoring party happening too which didn't help much. I was woken up very early again by the noise brigade and it seemed that the irritating family from day two were following me with their annoying habit. 'Let's get up at 5 a.m., to unpack, fold and repack' (for no reason!)

I was tired and extremely grumpy that day! Fortunately, it was an uneventful and easy days walk, planned around the usual food and drink stops. Mick and I left that day and walked with Jane and Orla. Although because Jane had a pair of lightening legs she waiting for us, for at least 20 minutes at each stop, until we'd catch up with her. Orla was semi-fast, but most of the time, she was slow enough to talk to.

That afternoon, we met a lovely guy called Craig, who is from the Lake District. He is an inspirational character to meet for all sorts of reasons, which I will explain later. We all walked together and came across what I think, was the most amazing stop I had during the whole of the Camino. Nestled in the forests at the top of the very steep mountain, was a great respite place from the extreme heat. There were hammocks swinging in the trees and a really nice woman, who had set up a table with all sorts of treats and more importantly at the time, some ice-cold drinks. We all stopped there for a long time, took our shoes off and relaxed.

It was a good job too because my left shin was starting to hurt! Not to mention the state of my feet, they looked disgusting and were painful! My new shoes were comfortable, but I was still getting the most terrible blisters. Mick had suggested, that I wear two pairs of woollen socks. One pair, to stop the friction and the other pair, to make my foot fit tightly in the shoe. Which I have now learnt is the worst idea ever!

Mick.. Mate, if you honestly didn't get any blisters? I think your feet must be made of stone!

Craig saved the day and gave me a pair of his cotton socks, which kind of sorted the problem. In hindsight, it was just such a bad decision to wear ankle high, heavy boots, dodgy branded shoes and woollen socks! Cotton socks and anti-blister ones definitely seem to be the best!

Belorado was a place that consisted of nothing special for me. We all stayed together, so there was a group of us, which was nice. We all had the usual cold showers and ate a revolting dinner from a cheap pilgrims menu. Which consisted of; a starter of some brown coloured dishwater that was supposedly soup; a strange chicken dish that wasn't cooked and served with some soggy, cold and undercooked chips and for afters a very bruised and slightly brown, apple.

The quality of the dinner didn't matter though, because of the rhyme, seen in several places along the way.

No Vino no Camino!

Never before, in the past ten days was it truer than that day. We sat in the afternoon heat of the sun, playing cards, laughing and joking and I think, between us all we drank around ten bottles of wine. Romance blossomed once again. Another girl I had met during last few days had chanced her arm and surprisingly made the first move and kissed me. When I set out on day 1 of the Camino the last thing that I ever thought about was, whether I would meet a nice girl and have a relationship and yet it happened to me twice in only 12 days. At the time, I thought that 'maybe I wasn't as fat, lumpy and unattractive as I thought I was.'

Days 13 - 16 – Belorado to Burgos

We were all very hung-over, walking away from Belorado and I'd had yet another average nights sleep again. The noise brigade was definitely following me. Although, this time there was a new member of their band. A sleep talker'er.. 'Hmmm sand and sea.' is what I heard him saying in the middle of the night. It happened twice too, so it wasn't a dreaming. Something to also be aware of: - the bunk beds. Particularly when you are drunk or hung-over. It can be very painful when trying to get down from the top bunk and slipping off the ladder, then landing badly on your foot and falling over. Although, it might be very amusing for other people to see.

The walk during the next few days from Belorado, was lovely as we all walked together and got on really well. It was extremely emotional though, because I was thinking about my dad a lot!

Arriving in Burgos was a relief, I was tired and my shin and foot were both hurting a lot, especially after the early morning bed incident. We found a lovely albergue to stay in, right by the Cathedral. I had a hot shower for a change and decided to dress up for some reason in a smart'ish sort of outfit. I guess it just felt like that kind of place. I went to sit on the terrace in the albergue to write my diary, while the others went off to have a drink in the bar opposite. While I was sitting there, I heard them talking about me, laughing at the state of my feet, falling out of the bed and how I should have the nickname;
Captain Hoppalong.

After I finished writing my diary, I went down to see them, one of them had asked for my cards, which I took with me. I threw them on the table when I got there and said, 'I heard what you said and I didn't think it was very nice.' So I walked away from them and found my own bar to have a drink and talk to a friend of the phone. After a while, I felt a lot better and went back to join the others and we ended up having a really good night. The next day, I was far too hung-over to do anything, so I stayed in Burgos and took a day off. Both my shin and feet needed it too!

Day 17 – Castrojeriz to Frómista

I cheated slightly and missed a stage by getting a bus to catch up with the guys and had a lovely evening with them when I got to Castrojeriz and the next day, we all walked together to Frómista.

When your 'job' for 30 odd days is to wake up at 6 a.m. put your clothes on, pack a bag and walk out the door only to spend the entire day walking, it is very strange not to do it. To only go as far as a kitchen to put a kettle on or walking to a station, somehow now feels very lazy.

So, it was great being back on the road again, especially after another days rest and having some luxury of staying in a hotel in Burgos. My shin and feet felt a lot better. It was good to be out in the open air and not in a city. It is definitely good for the heart, mind and soul to be out amongst nature.

During that day, we stopped in a café for the standard 'con leche' break and as we sat there, we saw some guy spraying his bag with a massive canister of pest repellent. It looked the type of stuff that could be, used to get rid of 'chinches.' Which in English means; bed bugs.

We all laughed about it and thought that it would be best to get away from him quickly, just in case there were any and wouldn't find their way to our bags, which were a bit too close to him than we wanted them to be.

Day 18 – Frómista to Carrión de los Condes

What a great day it was! I wasn't quite as hung over for a change, which made it slightly easier. We had lots more laughs and jokes between us all. Although, it was a sad day because Mick had gone ahead by train, as he wanted to skip the 'meseta,' which is the stage of the walk where the terrain is as flat as a pancake. There are barely any trees or places to hide from the heat of the sun that was bearing down on us all day! But, I loved it! The suntan I got and sweating some fat out from my skin during the day was brilliant!

We arrived relatively late in the afternoon and because it wasn't much of a drinking kind of place, we all had a night off drinking. We stayed in a convent with, the friendliest nun who greeted us when we checked in. We were each given a necklace of St Mary and a multi-coloured star-shaped piece of card. Every pilgrim that stayed there was given them as a blessing, to help on their journey.

After showering, having a lie-down and resting for a bit, we saw that the 'chinches boy' was sleeping in a bed next to Jane. We all had a lot of laughs winding her up, saying that she was going to get bitten. A few hours later, I cooked dinner for everybody and thought, that it was lovely spending time with all of them; we were just like a family.

After dinner, we all went to a guitar concert and a church mass afterwards. The concert was lovely, the sound of the guitar echoed all throughout the church. Afterwards, the mass was interesting, and it was a great service to see. Even though, I didn't understand all of it, having been to church enough times, I was able to work out what was going on.

During the mass, one of the girls got quite upset and started to cry, which made me feel emotional too and made me think about my dad and my epilepsy. At which point, another strange occurrence happened.

I was staring at a gold statue of Jesus that was behind the altar. When suddenly, a pigeon flew into the church through a window that was just above my head. It went right over the top of me and went and sat on the hand of the Jesus statue for a minute or so. It then flew around the church for a bit and went out the same window. I have no idea what or if any significance there is behind this but at the time it certainly helped to change my thoughts to happy ones and every time I think of it, it still does.

Day 19 – Carrión de los Condes to Terradillos

We all left together in the morning after a good nights sleep, but my word was my shin hurting. Orla took me to a Farmacia and I bought some 'Diclofenac' (ibuprofen) cream to try and help. Every time we stopped, I put a big dollop on my shin and every 4 hours I took some strong ibuprofen tablets. I think for most of the Camino. I was either, hung over or popping blisters and painkillers. I started to think of that process as a bit of slap (cream) and swallow (taking painkillers.) Which seemed to work.

When we arrived in Terradillos, we did all the usual things like showering, washing clothes, etc. Then I went and sat on a roof top terrace to do some first aid on all my wounds, sunbathe and write my journal. It was heaven! I had learnt from Mick that he had this method of measuring the quality of a burger, by the number of napkins needed. Therefore, after seeing burgers on the menu, I thought I'd test his theory. He seems quite right too. It took seven of those cheapo tracing paper style napkins to clean up the mess I'd made. I was a right mucky pup! I was pleased that it was just Craig and I sitting there and I didn't have to be prim and proper.

Things started to feel different in my head and heart while I was there. Coming up to the half-way mark, was a good feeling, I was thinking about the bird on the path, the magic lights, the pigeon, the motivational chats from Craig and how they all seemed to be having a positive effect on me. Either that or I was just very pleased not to be in London and working like a donkey anymore.

Day 20 – Terradillos to Sahagún

Craig was suffering from tendinitis too, so he stayed and took a rest day, so it was only four of us that walked on from there and during the day none of us spoke very much. I was listening to music a lot and was thinking about my dad and other things for most of the day. My shin was really hurting too! The cream was doing its magic, but I was getting used to it and it seemed less effective because I could still feel the pain.

After walking for only 2-3 hours, we arrived in Sahagún and I felt like I had done enough for the day and needed to rest. So, I decided that I was going to have an easy day and stay the night there. I tried to persuade the Irish to stay too, but because they didn't have time to complete the whole walk they weren't going to.

We went to an amazing art museum, where we found out, that they were giving away certificates to people to show how far they had walked. Afterwards, we went and had some final photos together at a big rock with a halfway plaque on it.

When we finished posing for photos, just as we were about to say goodbye, a van pulled up next to us, who was delivering bags to an albergue nearby. One of the girls was having her bag taken from place to place, when she saw it, she realised that it was the same company that she was sending her bag with. She went to see if the driver had it and it was there. So, she took it back and decided to stay the night with me. It was lovely to have the company and not be there on my own because I wasn't keen on the place.

Day 21 – Sahagún to El Burgo Ranero

When I woke up the next day, I felt refreshed and my shin was feeling a little better too. The friend that I was with left early by train, because she'd enough of the flat meseta and wanted to skip the rest and go straight on to Leon. After three, fabulous and funny weeks with some lovely people, it was sad to be on my own and in a one-man band again. It was an amazing feeling being part of a group and having such fun with them all.

Along the way, I stopped for a break in a farmyard type café. As it was another one of those sad feeling type of days, I treated myself to a big plate of bacon and eggs to cheer me up. Oh, how food can be so satisfying and make you feel instantly better! However, I realised, how much I missed proper English smoked back bacon from the butchers.

I got lost during the day because I'd lost sight of the yellow arrows. I was walking around in a hay field for ages, possibly even in circles. Until, I saw a farmer in his combine harvester who very kindly pointed me in the right direction. It was extremely hot and I was sweating buckets! I had a lot of banter with the guys in our Whatsapp chat, which helped keep me going a bit. The 'chinches' jokes seemed to be never ending!

My philosophy of, always having an end goal for each day was quite important. During the day I stopped lots of times because the pain in my left shin was unbearable, so I had to break that rule. After walking only 18 kilometres, I arrived in El Burgo Ranero, and thought, that it was far enough for one day! I found a lovely albergue and managed to get a comfortable private room for three people, which overlooked a beautiful garden. El Burgo, is a flat as a pancake farming style place, with pretty much nothing to it. It felt like the kind of town, where a traditional cowboy would feel right at home. It is a small town with only a handful of shops and bars. Strangely, it also felt like somewhere, that I had been to before?!

Craig decided to go for it that day and walk over 35 kilometres to catch me up, stay and walk together again. While I was on my own, I had a lovely lie down on a sun lounger to catch some sun. It was heaven relaxing, drinking some ice-cold beer and soaking my shin and feet in cold, salty water, until Craig arrived, at around 5'ish. We met a nice Italian chap, who I couldn't understand for the life of me, but we swapped some medicines and helped each other out which was nice. That night, he snored like a freight train and fidgeted like he had ants in his pants, which was a bit annoying. But, fortunately for me, he was in the bunk above Craig. Sorry mate!

Once again, it was another magical night. We had a nice cheap dinner in one of the only places to eat in the town and saw one of the most beautiful sunsets that I have ever seen. Looking out across the huge flat plain of land just in front of the albergue entrance. After the sun finally drifted away, it was such a clear night that the sky was full of stars! That song would have been very fitting at that moment. Craig and I were enjoyed a few bottles of wine and we met a nice guy called Fred.

We had a hilarious chat with him. Who, seemed to think that my voice and sense of humour deserves to be on television or the radio, or failing that I should work as a teacher. Fred also suggested that Craig should retrain to become a life coach/counsellor. Which ironically is exactly what I thought too and I am now very pleased to say, he is now retraining to be.

Having benefited from his wisdom, for over twenty-five days, I can safely say, that he is one of the best people to get advice from. Also, now knowing, how much he charges, I am very fortunate to have had it for free.

Thanks, Craig. I'll buy the wine next time!

Day 22 – El Burgo Ranero to Mansilla de las Mulas

A beautiful little place, where on the way in on the right there is an albergue and bar that has the most wonderful gardens. We stopped and sank a few beers there, before deciding whether to push on or to stay the night. In the end after three beers, we both realised that we were too tired and called it a day.

We found two beds in a place just over the road from where we were. It was a very nice albergue, owned by a friendly couple. It had a lovely kitchen, fabulous showers and the hottest garden that I have ever sat in. The weather was 42°C and sitting outside on a plastic garden chair, that was far too hot for my arse was not comfortable. What also didn't help was that the floor was made of that black children's playground type rubber. It felt like it was well over 50°C in there.

Day 23 – Mansilla de las Mulas to León

Craig and I, had a lot of banter between us all day, it was hilarious. To walk from place to place, on average would take between, 5-8 hours per day. Obviously, the time varied, depending upon the number of food and drink stops and for how long each one lasted. So it was impossible to talk to each other for that long, but with Craig and the others, it felt very easy and comfortable to chat for a bit, walk off alone or put some music on. Sometimes while I was walking on my own, I started singing my little heart out and rather randomly at least once or twice, both Craig and I were listening to the same song and singing it at the same time.

The day was the same as any other; we were up early with our bags packed; water bottles filled and boots on. We had also started to do some 'stretching,' and making sure that we had switched on the low battery mode, and turned the Wi-Fi off, on our phones. A further routine for me was; anything that had pain relief written on the label had either been slapped on my shin or swallowed. By this stage, I was used to the routine of walking and was a lot fitter and thinner than I was on day one!

We only walked 20 kilometres, still on flat pathways, so it was a really easy day, but when we arrived and I sat down, I realised how much my shin hurt! It was excruciating! Orla and Jane were there and had decided to stay and see us before they left for Santiago by train. Arriving in León was funny, both Craig and I were saying, 'Hola' to people just to be friendly and have a bit of fun. But we were, both ignored by everyone whom we said it to. Saying, 'Adios' didn't get a response either.

It was quite surreal meeting up with the girls it was almost like we were seeing old friends who we hadn't seen for ages. When in fact it was only a few days. The banter we exchanged in Whatsapp was hilarious, but the four of us in person was even better and had even more laughs. It was great to be half of whole a family again.

After we had said our goodbyes, Craig and I checked into a very cheap 20€, twin bed private room. I had spotted a spa on our way to the albergue and found out that it was only, 11€ to go in. I also saw a place offering, 'pilgrims massages.' So I made an appointment for later that afternoon because we went to relax and swim at the spa first, which was amazing! Every muscle and joint in my body felt so rejuvenated when we left. It was almost as if the last 23 days of walking, pain and suffering had been just a dream. The massage was with a chap called, 'Carlos' who I'm sure had magic massaging hands because after seeing him, my shin felt so much better! Although, I did have to sacrifice a lot of hair from my shin so that he could put some special tape on it.

We had dinner at a nice restaurant, sitting outside in a lovely garden. There were grape vines growing around an awning, which were swinging back and forth in the breeze. Scattered around the garden, there were also lots of pot plants with some wonderful smelling flowers. However, it felt slightly awkward, because sat at every table except ours, was a Spanish couple. We wondered whether Valentine's Day in Spain was in August. So we concentrated on drinking wine and eating some delicious food.

Day 24 – León to Hospital de Órbigo

Another lie in and another late start, it was approximately 11 a.m. by the time we eventually got going. It was also one of the hottest days that I remember! We walked around 15 kilometres in a well over 40°c heat with nothing but fields of sweet corn around us. Some of the fields had water spraying on them, which was very tempting to go and run through, but didn't, just in case, there were chemicals in the water. I think the most exciting part of that day, was when a flock of sheep was being shepherded past us.

Hospital de Órbigo is another beautiful old town. On the way into the town, there is a very big jousting lawn and a lovely bridge to walk over. It would be great fun to stay there for a while and see what goes on.

The albergue, we stayed was another nice place with more friendly owners. I think most of the 'hospitalero's.' Which is the name given to the people working in an albergue, were all very kind and friendly. There was a swimming pool nearby, which was incredibly refreshing to go in. Cold water, certainly works wonders on tired a tired and achy body. After we got settled, we were both so hot and thirsty, that we had a night off the vino and drank lots of cold water, iced tea and orange juice instead.

Day 25 – Hospital de Órbigo to El Ganso

Despite the rest and a hearty bacon and eggs breakfast, we were both very tired. We met a lovely old French couple, who were good to talk to for a while and inspired us to get going. The weather was terrible. It was raining on and off all morning. We stopped for a 'con leche' in Astorga and very nearly stayed because neither of us had much energy nor the drive to continue. There were also big black clouds and massive downpours of rain, which made the walk, seem a lot less appealing. It was a complete contrast to heat during the day before.

When the clouds finally cleared, our energy levels and the motivation to continue returned in us both, so we decided to soldier on and stick to our plan of walking the 32 kilometres to El Ganso. BUT, my word was it tough, the sun and heat, that afternoon was incredible and was definitely worse than every other day so far. Still, after lots of water and eating some frutos secos *(nuts and fruit)*. I felt full of energy and carried on.

El Ganso is famous because of the 'Cowboy bar,' which sadly was not the place for me and I don't think that Craig liked it much either! It was so dead and boring. The tiny village in the middle of nowhere was not much fun. We decided to stay there though because the next day was a walk with a very steep ascent in the morning and descent in the afternoon.

The albergue we stayed in was a small very quiet place and was really quite dull. We managed to get two of the last few beds available, in a very hot room with more than fifteen bunks in it and no windows. Craig and I put some washing on and relaxed in the garden while it was going round. After an hour, I went to see if it was finished and I thought it was, because there was no water in the machine. So, I opened the door and found out, that there was water in it and managed to upset the hospitalero, who turned out to be standing behind me, just as the water made a big puddle all over the floor. He was very angry and not impressed. It was very amusing though because his broken English was hilarious.

For the next part of our adventure, Mick had suggested that we stay in a place in Acebo, which had a lovely swimming pool. It was somewhere that he had stayed when he walked the Camino last year, been to again this year and found out that it was still just as good. Mick's recommendations of places to go are generally never too far off the money. Especially when it comes to burgers and places to eat. Most of the time, he will say, 'I've been there.'

Day 26 – El Ganso to El Acebo

This day was quite possibly, one of the longest and toughest days that I had, during the whole of my way on the Camino. Walking 25 kilometres, by this stage was relatively easy, but going up one of the steepest ascents, (1500m above sea level) throughout all of the Camino, it was far from it! What made it worse though, was the even steeper descent on a path that goes down through a river gorge before arriving in El Acebo. The walk to get there did wonders for the tendinitis, by the end of the day; I was suffering from it in both of my shins!

It was also, one of the most emotional days too, for it was the day where we encountered, **The Cruz de Hierro – The Iron Cross.**

The cross sits at the highest point of the Camino France and has been there since the 11th century. It is a great sight to see and a lot bigger up close than it is in a photo. The idea is that a pilgrim carries a rock with them and leaves it at the cross. This is meant to symbolise the sins that a pilgrim has committed in their life and the act of leaving it behind is supposed to absolve them of those sins.

As I have already mentioned. My reasons for doing the Camino journey were because I just really wanted to change my stars and live a happier life. But, what I realised when I arrived there. Was that the majority of my thoughts so far, had been about, my friends; my love life or lack there of both. Also how I wanted to live up to those words that I'd said to my dad before he died; how I felt when I had my epileptic fits and how much I missed him and my family. Strangely, I had even thought about my own death and realised how much I have to live for and grateful for.

Without gratitude and love in our lives, it can be very depressing. Which is exactly how I felt up until this Iron Cross – sad, alone, depressed, and I was missing my dad and family.

When he was ill, I found a small rock on the street one day. I put it into a heart-shaped tin, with red and white hearts printed on the outside and I gave it to him for good luck. Sadly though it obviously didn't work and sometime after he died, my mum gave it back to me. At the time I didn't know what to do with it, so I just put it in a drawer and forgot all about it.

Until one day, when my first girlfriend, the one who I was with when I had my epilepsy fits, introduced me to a self-help type of book, which talks of 'gratitude rocks.' After I read this chapter in the book, I remembered that I had this rock, so I decided to carry it around with me and tried to remember what I should be happy and grateful about. I felt like it didn't work because, in London, I always felt sad, grumpy, miserable, and lonely. I was generally just not very happy.

While I was researching the Camino on the Internet, I found out about the Iron Cross and the idea of leaving mementos there. I remembered about this rock and decided that that was going to be my offering to the collection. I carried it with me, safely tucked away with my passport and was very careful not to lose it.

When we got there, I realised that the cross is a lot bigger than it looks in photographs and is also a very emotional place to be. Seeing some of the poems and things that other people have left there, made me feel a lot more grateful for the things that I have in my life and has helped me to focus on the positives in life rather than the negatives. Craig and I stayed there quite some time, quietly thinking and reflecting.

When I walked away from the cross, there was a strange feeling; in my body like the air was blowing through me. The pressure that was on my shoulders was no longer there. I felt lighter if that makes sense. But also a great deal happier too. I can't explain what it was like, but it was an incredible feeling and since leaving there, I have never really had the same thoughts or feelings again. Obviously, I still miss my dad and would love for him to be around, to see me get married, have kids, etc. But he is here, in my head and my heart, which is a lot better place to be than not at all!

Another thing I learnt while I was there was that, god forbid, when the day does come and I die. That I want my funeral to be the same as my dads was, where the church is so full of people that, cared for him and loved him and that not everyone can fit in!

If there's one thing that I have learnt anything in my short life so far... Being a kind, hospitable, friendly, caring, honest and loving person is far, far better than being one who is depressed, angry, sad, lonely, upset and frustrated. Which are characteristics that my dad had and ones that I am now striving to be.

We all have the ability to change things that we don't want and it only takes a moment to take the first step and make the changes we want to come true.

El Acebo

Mick was quite right! The albergue is perched beautifully on the mountainside and is a hidden paradise with the most incredible views! It is a heavenly place to stay with very comfortable rooms.

The building is quite modern in design and similar to that of a Swiss-style skiing lodge. Outside there is a beautiful grassed area and a bar that serves the biggest bocadillo sandwiches and an amazing cold-water swimming pool. Oh.. and they also serve some lovely ice-cold white wine. Craig and I, spent several hours there, enjoying the wine, eyeing up the women and relaxing like kings instead of pilgrims. I think we were definitely on the 'Pampered Pilgrims' Camino way, rather than walking the 'pobre route.' We had another private room and an expensive dinner. Thinking about this now, it's no wonder why I spent so much money.

Out of all the places we stayed, if I had to choose one to return to, this would certainly be one of them. Although, if I did go there again. I definitely wouldn't want to be suffering with tendinitis in both shins and with feet that looked like quite as disgusting.

The best swimming pool and cold wine in El Acebo

Day 27 – El Acebo to Villafranca del Bierzo

After the luxury we had that night, I felt as fit as a fiddle when I woke up. Once again, the cold water in the pool had done the trick for the tendinitis and the rest in a comfortable bed had done me the world of good. Although just in case, I did my usual routine of slap and swallow. I could have quite easily have stayed there for a few days. But no, we made a plan and set off and gosh, what long day it was! We decided to forget the plan and walk further, because we both felt so fit and able and ended up walking 40 kilometres.

During most of the way, there is always a hill right at the very end of the day. Literally, just before arriving at a place, these hills or sometimes mountains, would be there just to well and truly, finish me off for the day properly. This day, was quite possibly one of the worst. I was wrecked with exhaustion by the time we arrived. It almost felt like the rest and relaxation in Acebo was all a dream and didn't happen.

We walked the last part into the town with a lovely girl called Luca from Hungry and a friend of hers. We had seen them on the way to El Acebo and had helped Luca out with some tape that I had in my first aid kit. Someone had stolen her shoes the day before, and had been given an old pair by the hospitalero working at the albergue she'd stayed in. The soles were peeling off, so we taped them back on for her so that she could continue her journey. They were both lovely to walk and talk and helped to distract me from how tired I was.

We arrived in Villafranca a 9 p.m., found an albergue and managed to get a four-bed room all to ourselves. It wasn't the cleanest of places though and seemed a bit like a mental intuition or prison. But neither of us cared very much because we were so tired, hot and hungry. We met a guy called 'Jesus' who joined us for dinner. He had the most random and scary stories of persecution and bad things that had happened to him. It was interesting but quite scary listening to him. That night, we drank three bottles of wine, ate a lot of food and went to bed, very drunk!

Day 28 – Villafranca del Bierzo to La Faba

What a long and very slow day this was, everything in my body hurt, I was exhausted and very hung-over! The blisters on my left foot were unbearable and no matter, what I did to them nothing seemed to make any difference. Until we got to a small village called, Vega de Valcarce, where there is a stream with lovely cold water. It was the perfect place to dip my manky feet in, relax and listen to some equally cold and chilled music. After stopping there, everything felt a lot better! The water had reduced the swelling of my feet and even made my blisters feel a lot better. While I was sitting there, I spoke to Rachel, who had recommended a place to stay in, La Faba. But I couldn't remember what it was called or where exactly she'd said it was. It was great to hear from her and surprise her with how far I had walked and how determined I was to continue!

The weather during the day was around 38°c, so it was another very hot day! The closer we got to La Faba, the more I feared impending doom of the end of day hill or mountain and I can tell you, this one was horrible. It was very rocky, steep and because it was so hot it was bloody hard work! I had to stop at least five times to drink some water and breath. My lungs probably sounded like a steam train whistle all the way up there.

The albergue that Rachel had recommended was incredible. A young and very friendly couple ran it. There was a very calming and relaxing feel to the place. The beds were in a high vaulted almost barn-like room and were very comfortable! While Craig and I were enjoying our end of the day drinks, we saw that girl called Luca walk past. I called her over to say hi, so she stopped and talked to us. Craig managed to persuade her to stay, which was great because we all got on so well. I thought to myself that she looked more exhausted than I felt!

That night we ate a delicious vegetarian dinner. Which never before have I eaten a meal without meat and enjoyed it as much as I did. Although for now, it still hasn't converted me to stop eating, roast beef with all the trimmings or a smoked bacon sandwich.

Day 29 – La Faba to Triacastella

Another challenging day that started with a steep climb followed by an even steeper descent. My severely blistered feet and tendinitis shins were in absolute agony. Still, Craig and I walked on with Luca and some other guys who she'd met a few times during her journey. It seemed like we were forming a new group.

Triacastella is a very relaxing town with a selection of lovely looking albergues to stay in. It is also another place where you can stay in a private room too. I think this was probably my sixth or seventh and that's not including the two hotels that I stayed in either. It is also a great place to sort out one's blisters because it's a flat town and the Farmacia fortunately, isn't too far to go to.

My technique for dealing with blisters, which has worked perfectly well before, but wasn't very intelligent at all this time. Was to pop it with a sterilised needle, then the next day, after all the liquid had drained out, I would cut the skin off. Which basically left an open wound. So imagine, three or four of these per foot. In hindsight, this method was really quite stupid.

The lady in the 'Farmacia' looked quite sick when I took my sock off and showed her. They were quite disgusting and I can still visualise what they looked like. I finally got them sorted out once and for all. I had a lot of criticism from a French chap who was staying in the same albergue. He apparently said to Craig, that I would be very ill when and if I finish the Camino. 'Ce n'est pas beau ugghhhh.' Is a phrase that will always remind me of him and the pretty garden where I was sitting and trying to relax, while drinking a cold beer, soaking my feet in some lovely cold and salty water.

Day 30 – Triacastella to Sarria

What a sad day this was, I was losing my wingman. Craig had left early to walk the last few days on his own. I'd made such a strong bond, sharing experiences, laughs and jokes with him that it was all of a sudden, very strange to be walking without him. So, I ended up walking with Luca instead. Walking with her was very different. We didn't have much banter going on and only talked together briefly, before walking in our own little worlds. Halfway through the day, we saw the others that we'd met, and stopped to join them in a lovely hippie style meditation place. It was a heavenly spot to sit, relax, drink extremely strong coffee and I have a swing in a hammock.

I thought that the walk leading us into Sarria, was pretty bleak and dull, it seemed very similar to a council estate. As you can probably guess, I was also suffering in so much pain in my shins again. They both needed a very good rest! Luca and I were going to stay the night there together, but she didn't like the town at all and changed her mind. We walked through and up some very steep steps to leave when she changed her mind again and decided that we stay. So we went back down the to the bottom of the steps in search of an albergue. My, how I hated her for that because every step I took up and then down was excruciating!

Fortunately, there was a place to stay very close to the bottom of the steps, so we didn't have to walk too much further. They had two beds for us, right next to a window, which was great because the room was packed. After the usual end of the day routine; which by now was like second nature, consisted changing; showering; stretching; washing clothes and doing my medicinal, slap and swallow. I found out there was a place that did massages. So I organised one and had my other shin sorted out. It meant more shaved hair though. My shins must have looked so ridiculous. As you can tell, tendinitis in both shins wasn't pleasant!

That night, neither of us felt very energetic or wanted to spend much money. So, I went and bought some food for us in a local supermarket and we had a picnic sitting in the living room in the albergue. Of course, we had some nice red wine too. We then retired to the garden to have a smoke and finish what was left of the wine. I started to play some music on my phone to keep us entertained. Which seemed to be a good thing, because she started to sing to one or two songs that I had chosen.

Now I can tell you, never before in any moment of time have I heard such a glorious voice. I got goose pimples all over me from listening to her! Whenever I listen to music with someone else and then listen to music on my own. I can always remember the person I was with, by the songs I was listening to when we were together. Anytime I hear these same songs now; it instantly reminds of her and that situation. Sitting there in that garden at that moment was a phenomenal ending to what was a very tough and challenging day!

Day 31 – Sarria to Portomarín

When I woke up, I didn't have much energy and didn't want to go very fast, so Luca and I split up and walked separately. Naturally, I was alone again and I had the same thoughts and feelings of loneliness. To get through it and push on, I just listened to my music and sang my heart out. Which seemed to do the trick, because I met a lovely couple from Barcelona, who were laughing their heads off at my singing. They were very funny and great company, also because I could practice speaking Spanish with them too. In the end, I'd had enough and it became a bit much trying to talk to them and I got the feeling that they wanted some 'couples' time. So I wished them a 'Buen Camino' and walked on relatively quicker and with a quieter singing voice. In the next town, called Morgade, I decided to stop in a charming little coffee shop for a 'con leche' and some slap and swallow. While I was sitting there, I saw the couple again and they came over and joined me for a drink, which was lovely. It turns out that my Spanish isn't actually all that bad.

We were having a nice chat and then out of the blue, Luca sent me a message on Facebook asking me, 'if I had her knife?' I rummaged around in my bag to see if I could find it but, alas, no, it wasn't there. She must have left it in the albergue that we'd stayed in the night before. She told me that she was only 1.4 kilometres away in the next town and asked, 'if I wanted to, I could catch up and walk with her.' So I did and made some new friends who she'd met while she was there and we all left together. I was very happy about that too because this stretch of the walk marks the last five days before arriving in Santiago de Compostela and there's a marker for the last 100k. She was just the person that I wanted to be with there and I feel very lucky to have met her and enjoyed her company. I also cannot believe how good I look in the photos. I had lost a lot of weight and was very tanned!

Luca and I at the 100k remaining marker

As this walk is meant to be a pilgrimage style journey, it seems unfair, that it is possible to walk the last stretch of 100 kilometres and still be eligible for a certificate in Latin when arriving in Santiago de Compostela. Amongst the group we'd now formed, we called these people all sorts of different names; some were polite and some not so nice. Two of them are, 'holiday pilgrims or tour'agrinos.' But my personal favourite though was;

'I bet you're going to be suffering from blisters and bad feet by the time you arrive at the Cathedral in Santiago!'

After the marker, because I was walking so slowly, Luca and I had split up again. By the time I arrived at the town of Portomarín on my own, I was feeling very tired, sorry for myself and was still suffering in pain. I felt happy that there were only a few days left because my shins needed a proper rest. Although, I didn't want my way to end!

Before finding somewhere to stay for the night, Luca and another new friend I'd made were walking past, they came and said, 'hello, and explained how they were both going to walk on.' So we said our goodbyes and I went off to get myself sorted. I felt very sad saying goodbye to them because for the first time in 30 days I was staying the night on my own. I couldn't quite believe how fast the time had flown by.

After I had a shower and washed my clothes, I went outside to hang them up and have a smoke in the garden. Afterwards, I was about to have a lie-down, when suddenly, Luca wandered in and said to me, 'Surprise! I decided to stay too.' Unfortunately, she couldn't stay in the same Albergue, because it was full, so she had got a bed in the place just over the road. It was funny that she was there because after she had left me earlier, I had gone and bought her a new knife to replace the one that she'd lost.

There is a very big bridge to cross on the way to Portomarín. From which, we saw that there might be a place to swim in the river. After buying some beers, Luca suggested that we go down to have a look. When we got down there, we saw that there were other people who had, had the same idea. They also just so happened to be, two of the other guys that we had met a few days back. It was such fun!

I had a good night there. I met that funny couple from Barcelona again and I met a nice French girl. There was a big group of us all sitting and having dinner and a few drinks together. It was a great ending to a very good day.

Day 32 – Portomarín to Eirexe

I hadn't seen any of the others in the morning, so I'd left on my own, but I didn't mind for a change because, at the time, I wanted to walk the last few days on my own. The walk itself was lovely in the morning until the tendinitis in my shin began to hurt! It was unbearable and I think it was actually getting worse. My slap and swallow technique of cream and pain killers was no longer working, even having stepped up the drugs to 1000mg of Paracetamol, instead of the 600mg Ibuprofen. I considered taking a bit of both to see if that would help, but I wasn't brave enough.

After a few hours, I had to stop to rest and buy some more cigarettes. I found a nice place called the Labrador bar, which was a great place to stop for a while and sunbathe in the little garden. The food looked good too, but I couldn't cope with eating anything. I just sat there with ice on my shin, feeling very unhappy and sorry for myself. I was also very angry too because they didn't have a cigarette machine and the next one was a good 2 hours walk away! There was no way that this was going to stop me. I was going regardless of the pain.

Eventually, I had built up enough courage and got going. I was doing ok for the first part of the walk until the terrain changed from an easy path to a walk down through a rocky-river bed and a steep gorge. The pain in my shins was incredible. On my way down, an Italian gentleman asked me, 'if I was ok, and if I needed some help?' I replied, 'that I felt like an old man.' To which he told me, 'I already am an old man, but here take my arm.' Walking down this gorge was very difficult and every step I took was excruciatingly painful.

While we were walking, he was trying to distract me from thinking about my shin, by having a lot small talk. After I had told him all about me, I asked him the same questions. He turned out to be 78 and was walking the Camino because he wanted to do it before he got too old. He also said that he was a designer of children's clothing brand for one of the most well-known stores in the world, based in London. Considering his age, I feel very grateful and lucky to have had his help for a while. He was very kind and I cannot thank him enough.

However, his suggestion upon parting that I take a taxi haunted me for a very long time after he'd left. Every time the temptation part of my brain was caving in, a taxi would drive past. Eventually, when I arrived in the town where the blessed cigarette machine was meant to be. I found out that there wasn't one but there was.. A bloody taxi rank with four cars waiting instead. At that moment, I thought to myself, 'come on Matt, left leg, right leg and the other one will follow.'

Come hell or high water. I was going to get there! Eventually, when I did finally arrive at the next bar, I found out that they didn't have a cigarette machine either! I was really cranky, but very determined to carry on. I was trying a different technique to ignore the pain and it worked too, because I achieved my goal for the day and walked the 18 kilometres that I wanted to. I found another bar and a place to stay and decided to give up on my smoking quest. It was a very peaceful place and it seemed a better idea to rest my legs! I put some ice on my shins and slept in the garden all afternoon.

The pension albergue I stayed in was lovely and is worth staying in if you are ever in the neighbourhood! The lady will even wash your clothes and fold them for you, and do it for only 4€ too! The bar opposite served me a delicious, six napkin rated burger and chips and I had a bottle of wine to celebrate my achievement of getting there. Feeling full and content, I went inside to pay and surprise surprise inside on the left as I went in, there was a cigarette machine. I was a happy boy after seeing that!

I stayed to have another drink or two and realised how much I was missing all of the friends I'd made and the thought of being only three days from the end was a very strange. I needed a rest, but I didn't want it to end. I spoke to my best mate from Madrid and my sister. It was lovely to hear their friendly voices although it made me feel homesick. But I was very pleased to be where I was at that moment and not be at home. I started to formulate an end of Camino plan, of going to Madrid, to visit my friend for a weekend, before going on to Mallorca to get a job on a yacht.

Day 33 – Eirexe to Melide

I had another private room in the albergue and had a great nights sleep! The rest had done the trick once again. After the usual morning routine, I set off with a plan to walk a 23-kilometre day. I was determined to get to Santiago even if I had to crawl the remaining way there! I think the walking sticks I had were under a lot of pressure. I remembered my mum's advice and took it slow and steady. I saw Luca along the way, she waved at me, but I didn't stop, which was possibly a bit rude, but I was on a 'captain hoppalong' hobble and had a rhythm of forward motion going on and wasn't going to stop.

The feelings of loneliness that I'd had during the past 30 days had subsided slightly and I didn't care about it anymore. In fact, it was and it still is nice to be on my own. Lost in my own thoughts enjoying whatever sights and sounds may be around, undisturbed and uninterrupted. Along the way, I met a nice couple from Canada, who I think felt sorry for me because the lady gave me some of her extra strong prescription painkillers. Which, I feel bad that I didn't take, but I didn't want them to have an adverse effect with my epilepsy medicine. I thought that would really take the 'Michael' if I were to fall on the floor, flap my arms around, bite my tongue lots and have a fourth fit. Especially being in the middle of nowhere and so close to the end.

Shortly after seeing Luca, I saw another bar, so I decided it was time to have a rest. I was thinking about how I was a bit rude to her and thought that perhaps I should have stopped. But, when I walked in to the bar, I saw that somehow, she was already there. It doesn't make sense how that would be possible either because I didn't see her walk past me? Anyway, I asked the guy who was working behind the bar for ice and explained why. So he went off out the back and rather than coming back with some, he gave me a big and fat sirloin steak instead. He told me to put it on my shin with it elevated and if after ten minutes it didn't feel better, then he would give me some ice.

I walked away from the bar thinking rude words in my head because all I wanted was some ice. However, after having some food and something to drink, I felt ready to go. I decided to forget about the ice and put some deep heat and ibuprofen cream on it. When I stood up and walked to the bar, to give the steak back. I couldn't quite believe it because it felt like I had a brand new shin?! I suddenly felt awful for thinking all those nasty thoughts I'd had. In reality, I bet that he regularly gives a piece of steak to people, for the same reason.

Luca and I left and walked together for a while until we split up again because I was going so slowly. I caught up with her a bit further on, but I didn't want to stop again. She blew me a kiss, which was lovely, but it wasn't enough for me to go over and sit down. I was on a roll and wasn't going to stop for anything. I had to do a long day if I wanted to get to Santiago on time and be able to go to Madrid for the weekend.

I reached my target place for the day at 5 p.m. I picked an albergue to stay in and managed to get a bottom bunk by a window, which was very happy about. Mainly because most of the rooms that I'd stayed in, smelt of feet and sweat. So it was great being able to control the ventilation for a change.

I had a lovely shower and had a first aid session with my feet. The lady in the Farmacia in Triacastella had given me some Iodine to put on my blisters. While I was sat on my bed trying to put it on, it seemed to just go everywhere other than the places where it was meant to be going. It was quite frustrating, but in the end, I'd had enough and it was time for the routine end of day drink. I left the hostel and went to a nice bar not too far away, sat and iced my shins, aired my feet and wrote my diary. When I'd finished and all the ice had melted, I decided to go for a walk around find somewhere else to have dinner. After an hour of 'hoppaling' round the town looking for somewhere, I became quite cross and grumpy because I hadn't found anywhere that I liked the look of. So in the end, I just went back to the same bar.

I ordered a burger and some aioli chips and a large glass of red. Now, as a burger and chips go; this one was incredible. It was a nine napkin burger! It was so big; I couldn't even get mouth around it. The bit I liked the most, was that it was all wrapped in a seeded bun, with the top cut out so that the egg yolk could wink at me when it was put on the table in front of me. The chips were amazing too, plenty of delicious alioli and it was the biggest bowl. I was very full and content!

After dinner, I got into bed early slightly wine pickled and was starting to doze off straight away. When suddenly, a woman also staying the night in the room screamed her head off. An Italian chap jumped out of his bed, spoke to her in Italian loudly and then started waving his torch around. After he'd room turned into a Melide disco everyone, including me was awake. Apparently, she had spotted something on the wall above and on her bed. She thought they were; Chinches! – Bedbugs. I thought to myself, 'oh dear.. All my jokes are backfiring and now it's my turn to be taunted!' All of us were kicked out of the hostel, for 2 hours. The owners fumigated the room with a special spray. We were eventually allowed back in at around 2 a.m. Although I am not quite sure, I think that I was bitten that night. Chinches are famous for biting in a straight line and leave behind red traces as a mark of their fury. The reason why I am not sure is because I only noticed a few days later that I had such a line, but it didn't seem too bad, so I don't think I was 'chinchossed.'

Day 34 – Melide to O Pedrouzo

It was my penultimate day and I felt exhausted! After the chinches debacle, I only slept for four hours. I had to have a few coffees before leaving just to give me that extra oomph to go. During my very slow walk, I met some Irish women who kept me company for a while. One of them said, that I was very handsome. She was a nice lady, but she was far too hand'sy and forthcoming for my liking so, I had to use one of my great ideas and say;

'I'm sorry ladies, but I have to push on because I'm meeting a friend in the next town.' I then wished them a Buen Camino and walked away quickly! I didn't want to have another relationship with anyone, particularly with someone in the plus 55-age bracket.

Fortunately, my white lie about meeting someone came true when I saw Luca in the next town. I went to chat with her, but she wasn't very talkative and walked off on her own. I figured that perhaps it was karma for me having ignored her twice. Part of the walk went through a peaceful woodland. I stopped and drank a nice coffee from a woman selling things from the boot of her old Citroen CV. I met a nice lady, who agreed with Fred, who I met in El Burgo. That I should think about changing my career from hospitality to becoming a teacher or doing something on the television or radio. I didn't tell her that someone else had already said that to me either.

After a while of chatting to her, I walked on my own and I was quite happy. Tomorrow was going to be the last day and I thought that I wanted to be going it alone. However, Luca had caught up with me and was staying the night in the same place as me, but we didn't talk very much. I had made some new friends and was heading out for some drinks and food with them, only to be ditched by them five minutes after. Fortunately, Luca and her friends were there and they invited me over. It was lovely, sitting there together, making new friends and playing a few rounds of my favourite card game. Which is also one that I must have taught to hundreds of people by now, it's called: - 'Shit head.'

Day 35 – O Pedrouzo to Santiago de Compostela

The end was in sight; it was finally my last day and my last 20-kilometre walk. I was shattered and still suffering with bad shins and blisters, but I really didn't want my way to end. It was one of the best experiences of my life so far ever and I am very pleased and proud of myself for doing it.

Luca and all the others that I had met during those last few days had left earlier than me, so just as I wanted, I was on my own. I was ambling along because I didn't want to rush and more to the point, I couldn't go much faster anyway. I stopped a few times to put some ice on my shin and drink a coffee and at one stop, I drank an iced coffee just to mix things up a bit. I was reflecting on everything that had happened to me in my life up until that point; being bullied at school; my dad dying and the surrounding circumstances, my epileptic fits; working too much; my lack of social and love life. Then, I was thinking about the amazing journey that I had just been on and suddenly I felt a strange feeling of calmness but also a great deal of sadness that the day and my way and was coming to an end. I then started to think about the people I'd met and how much fun it was to share the experience with different people and make some new friends.

After a while, I saw a guy selling all sorts of touristy tat. There was a big bunch of holiday pilgrims, who it seemed were mostly walking in a lot worse state than I was. Which, being slightly cruel, I was quite pleased about. 'Go and do the whole thing I thought.' But anyway, I browsed around this tourist trap and saw that he was also doing credencial stamps. Which by this stage for me, it was a must! As much as my determination to finish, I wanted to fill up a second book of stamps. What I failed to realise until the last week, was that can collect two a day and fill up your book so you can show off at all the places you've been to. Which, is something else, I wished that I had known at the beginning. Not that the blisters and hobbling wasn't enough proof. So, there I was getting a stamp when the guy tried to flog me a walking stick. I said, 'no thank you,' because I already had my own.

As I was walking away from the tat trap, I started thinking about my latest group of friends and that I didn't want to be walking alone. Particularly on the last day, and then I thought about that guy giving away the stick, 'he was very pushy.'

Then it suddenly dawned on me, that the stick looked remarkably like Luca's. For the next 15 minutes or so after leaving there, the thought that it might be hers, was playing on my mind and whether I should go back and get it or not. I doubted that she would have left it like that because she seemed very attached to it. While I was ambling along, I noticed a white hoodie style jumper hanging from a tree branch. It looked very similar to the one that Luca wore quite often. However, it was pretty grim, so I thought no.. it can't be hers.

Having seen this second sign, I was about to turn around to go back to get it, in case fate would bring us together again. When sure enough, who did I see running towards me? Luca! I was so relieved to know, that I wasn't going mad, thinking that the stick was hers but also because it was lovely to then have some company.

After the best hug and cuddle, we walked and talked together for a while and then were soon in our own separate worlds again, but at least we were together. Knowing that there is a friend either in front or behind is a lovely feeling. When we arrived in the next town, all of the others that who we'd met the last few days were there. We all sat together in a big group, which was lovely. In fact, it was a magical moment because we all got on so well and had such a laugh. We sat there for ages before eventually deciding to walk on.

During the last hour, I was walking with a lovely girl from Slovakia. She was asking me the standard questions and then she asked me the big one; 'Why was I walking the Camino?' After everything I had thought about, the pain I'd suffered, the Iron Cross, etc. The only answer I could give her was;

I've done it for my.. Dad

Santiago de Compostela

Now if ever there is a time, that I have been pleased to arrive somewhere, this was one of them. I didn't want to stop, but I seriously needed a rest! There is a long walk before getting to the famous Cathedral. I was still walking with my new Slovakian friend. But we'd stopped chatting because I'd decided that I wanted to listen to a song, while we walked the last 5 minutes or so before arriving at the Santiago signpost. The song that I wanted to listen to was from an album that my mum and dad would always listen to.

Frank Sinatra, Duets II and the song – My Way.

The fact that the walk is also called the 'Way' is coincidental.

Within seconds of listening to the song, I burst into tears and almost fell over. My latest friend ran straight over, stopped me from falling and gave me a big kiss and a cuddle. Which cheered me up a bit and brought me back to reality!

After a few photos with the Santiago sign, we went to the nearest bar for a celebratory drink. Afterwards, we went and saw the Cathedral. Which was another emotional moment for me, the thought that I…

'Fat Matt' had eaten, drunken, smoked, hopped and hobbled my way from France and all across the northern coast of Spain had walked over 750 kilometres and completed the Camino! The prayer that I made on day 1, for my hip & knee not to hurt had worked because they didn't hurt once! The pain in my shins, more than made up for it instead.

We sat in the main square drinking a few more beers, before going for a look around the Cathedral. We then went and got a stamp in our credencials and collected our Latin certificates. After that was done, we had another drink and made a joint decision, let's keep going and go to 'The End of the World, in Finisterre.' The official end of the Camino is next to a marker that says 0.00k.

The famous Cathedral
My certificate in Latin

On the final road into Santiago de Compostela

Finisterre

Despite our determination to go onwards, we all decided that we'd had enough walking and took a bus to Finisterre instead. It was very strange, sitting on a bus for a few hours after spending so much time outdoors and not using my feet to take me somewhere. We had bought some beers and played some music to keep us entertained. Just for an extra bit of fun, we had a singsong to some silly songs like, 'wheels on the bus' too.

We arrived at around 8 p.m. and were all very glad to get off the bus. I felt a bit cramped and claustrophobic while I was on it. We went to find a place to stay, dropped our bags off and bought some beers and then searched for a beach and the sea to swim and 'cleanse' ourselves and properly end our Camino 'Way's.' When we got to the beach, I stripped off in seconds and ran straight into the sea. It was one of the most glorious feelings, 9 o' clock at night, diving into the freezing cold Atlantic, suffering with the worst tendinitis and the most disgusting blisters. I didn't care about any of the injuries either because despite all the challenges, the ups and downs, the pain and suffering, I had finally done it!

After swimming for ages, we went and sat on some rocks overlooking the bay, drank some more beers and smoked a few cigarettes. Nobody said very much either, because there just wasn't anything to say. We all had made it and all felt very grateful, relieved and extremely elated!

The next day, I bumped into the friend I'd made on day 2. We walked up to the 0.00k marker and lighthouse together. Just like every end of the day place, it is also right at the top of a big hill, which is hard work to go to in the mid-afternoon September sunshine! I was dripping with sweat when I got to the top! I felt sad seeing the final marker and officially ending my journey. My friend and I sat there for a long time and took some amazing photos. On the way back to the town, I met four lovely girls from Genoa in Italy and we got on really well, we had some drinks and went to the beach together the next day.

Reflecting on my travels and feeling elated at seeing the 0.00k

Santiago de Compostela (for the second time)

I'd had a great time relaxing at the beach, catching up with Craig and Mick and again drinking a lot. But, it was sadly time to say goodbye and for the next chapter of my journey to begin. My plan was to go to Santiago to see the mass in the Cathedral and then go by train to Madrid for the weekend before flying to Mallorca and meeting up with a yacht crewing agency and getting a job.

I left Finisterre, very early in the morning, because I wanted to have some time to drink a coffee and have something to eat before going to the Cathedral. But, when I arrived I was a bit late and didn't have much time to faff around. I walked very quickly to get there on time because I didn't want to miss it.

When I walked into the Cathedral for the second time, I felt very emotional and cried my little heart out again and guess, who happened to be behind me at the time? It was the four Italian girls. Once again, I was given another great big hug and surprisingly another big kiss too, which as always instantly made me feel better. I love a good hug and a cuddle and may have been a teddy bear in a former life.

It was an incredible experience to have walked all the way across the north west of Spain through, mountains, fields and forests then ended up at the seaside. Then ending it with the mass in the Cathedral was simply amazing.

At the end of the mass, there is a chalice that gets filled with incense and is then swung over the top of the congregation. Which is a magical sight to see! Watching the rope swing, the people swinging it and the incense wafting through the air above me was incredible. I took a video of this part of the ceremony, and whenever I watch it or even think about it now, it still makes me feel slightly tearful but extremely grateful.

Madrid

I had said goodbye to my new friends from Genoa at the train station. I was going to Madrid by train. The journey was going to take five hours, which was the longest period of time that I had spent on a train since I'd left London. I felt very uncomfortable being in a confined space and had to walk around a lot and spend lots of money on food to distract my mind from where I was.

I'd met a lovely woman on the train, whom I practiced speaking Spanish with and she had spoken to her husband about giving me a lift to the place I was staying in. She was great company and distracted me from the claustrophobia that I felt while I was on the train. However, I was very relieved to arrive and get off the train and get out into the fresh air again.

I'd rented an apartment to stay in for the weekend. As soon as I walked in the door, I knew that I didn't like it. It just felt really dirty, the kitchen was disgusting, the bedroom was up a steep spiral staircase, in the roof of the building and the filthy and smelly bathroom was squeezed into the corner of the living room just under the stairs. The bedroom basically consisted of a mattress on the floor and was in the roof of the building, so the ceiling was so low that it was impossible to stand up. I had to crawl over to from the staircase to get into the bed, which was very annoying and painful.

But, what made it more irritating, was that the light switch was just above the bed, so I had to crawl over there on all fours, turn the light on and then do the same in reverse to turn the downstairs one off. I tried not doing this, but I couldn't see a thing as it was pitch black and ended up bashing my head on the roof. I felt a bit like a bat being in a cave.

In the end, it was fine for the weekend because I was only ever in there to sleep. The night I arrived, my friend came and met me at this apartment and took me out and for some drinks and dinner. She had chosen an awesome restaurant, where we sat on these big cushions in a sandpit and ate some delicious Mexican/American type food. After dinner, we went exploring on her motorbike and my friend showed me some of the famous places in Madrid.

My first day waking up in a proper bed even just a mattress on the floor was heaven. It was dark, quiet and very relaxing. I woke up refreshed and decided that I want to buy some new clothes. My friend had told me how to get to 'Gran Via' which is a big street with all the shops. I took a walk up there, which was nice and went to the cheap blue label boutique.

When I walked into this shop, I realised that it was huge! I went up 4 or 5 escalators before getting to the menswear department. By the time I got to the top, I felt like I was about to have a panic attack. There were just too many people in one place and it really stressed me out and made me feel uncomfortable. Fortunately, right behind me was a fire escape and a staff goods lift. I didn't care though; I ran into the life and got out of there, quick sharp. I went and hid in a coffee shop nearby until I'd calmed down. Then I sat on bench in a quiet street, smoking a few cigarettes. I had to give up the clothes buying idea in the end because I didn't want to go through that again.

By Sunday afternoon, I decided to stay another week. I decided to stay in another apartment because after such a long time of hearing the noises of other people, I wanted my own space. The place I had booked to stay in was amazing. It was a lovely small, clean and comfortable apartment, it was also in a perfect location, right near the centre of Madrid and the Plaza Mayor. My mate showed me around a lot more, I met some of her friends, had dinner with her mum and brothers at their apartment and I fell in love with the city.

At the end of that week, I decided to stay a bit longer, but I had some serious conditions. My money was running out, so I had to find a job and it had to be a job that started straight away too. I checked into a hostel that was as cheap as chips and was very comfortable. I met lots of friendly people and had a good time. One person, I met even gave me the same advice as Fred and the other lady, get a job as a teacher or work on the Television, News, and Radio.

Anyway, my conditions for of staying or going home were.

- Get some teaching qualifications (I thought; let's see if I like it)
- Find a job
- Get a bank account
- Sort out a National Insurance and, or Social Security number
- Ensure I could stay and work

By Friday of that week, I had succeeded on all of the above and found it was surprisingly easy too. All it took was a bit of effort and a lot of patience. Waiting in a lot of long queues, trying to speak and understand Spanish was the only difficult part.

Life for me was continuing to be very different. I was living in a city that I had only visited once, over ten years ago with some friends. Living away from home is fine, but living in a foreign country to do a new job was tough, but an amazing new experience and something I felt like I wanted and needed to do.

The job I found, was working for a Language Academy as a teacher. It seemed like it would be great fun, but I was put under a lot of pressure to follow their method of teaching in what felt like a very intense and restrictive atmosphere. Their method was quite basic; everything was taught using a T.V screen and a lot of questions. I didn't have any proper training and didn't feel very confident, so I am not surprised, but after four days of being thrown in at the deep end. I was basically told to go away, but if I wanted to come back when I had more experience, they would give me a trial shift and if I were good enough second time around they'd give a job.

I met a great bunch of people in the hostel I stayed in, regularly shared food, drink 1€ litre bottles of beer, smoke a lot and played cards. It was great fun sitting there with some of the people I met. We would play for hours. I was still making new friends and it felt very satisfying. It was a great feeling staying in a place with such nice people.

Considering the idea of being a teacher, I found a place that was offering a teaching a course called a CELTA (Cambridge Certificate of English Language Teaching to Adults). The course ran from October to December. It was very interesting, but gosh, was it tough!

Firstly, because I hadn't studied anything for over than ten years, it was hard getting used to the bright lights of a classroom and having to use my hands to write instead of serving plates of food or pouring drinks. Then there was my accommodation situation. I was living in a 4-bed room in a hostel, trying to type essays on the rooftop balcony, lying on the bunk bed, trying to read textbooks. But, what made it even more difficult for me was the need to have to work and earn money, on top of going to the lectures, writing essays, etc., was extremely challenging!

However, I thought, 'that if I can walk so far across this country, then I sure as hell can do all this and survive.' So I just got on with it and fortunately survived and passed. The other reason, why I had to get a job, is because I'd realised that I couldn't rely on using my credit cards anymore. They had been swiped so many times, that the black bar on the back of the cards was fading and there wasn't much money left to spend.

When I had finished the course in December, I had found a place to live. I was very lucky, because the manager in the hostel had recently bought a flat, refurbished it and agreed to rent a room to me. It was heaven to have checked out of the hostel and finally be living somewhere permanent like a normal person. However, I was seriously starting to doubt my new life of being a teacher and living in Madrid any more. I barely saw my friend, because she was always busy. So I started to feel very alone again and I was missing the walking and the camaraderie with the friends I'd made.

The week before Christmas, I met up with my friend for dinner. She mentioned that a friend of hers knew about a job that was available. She had said that she wasn't interested, but she had given her friend my phone number, so that she could ask me. I was desperate for money, some experience, and someone to just give me a chance, so I jumped at the opportunity and asked this friend of hers to put me in touch with the school.

On the 19th December 2016, I was heading home to London for Christmas. While I was sitting in the airport waiting to board, I was considering the idea of not returning to Madrid after Christmas! When suddenly, I received a message from my friends, friend, with the contact details of the person, I needed to speak to, who turned out to be a lady working for the Department of Education. I e-mailed her my C.V and received a reply from her straight away. She asked for a copy of my passport. Which was easy, as it was in my hand; I took a photo and sent it to her.

When I arrived in London, my mum was there to pick me up. It was good to see her and have another hug, the best of them all though; a good old mummy hug. After leaving the airport, we went to a local supermarket. While we were in the shop, I checked my e-mails to see if I'd had any replies. I had an e-mail asking me to rename all of the documents that I'd sent so far, and resend them. So, as soon as I got home, I did what I needed to and returned them. After maybe half an hour, I had received another reply. This time, it read: 'Go to the school on the 9th January.' I finally had some success and had something worth going back for.

I had a great Christmas while I was at home, seeing and spending time with my family and getting some good presents. It was perfect timing for me too because I needed some new socks and shower gel.

Continuing my new path of life in 2017

It was a great feeling returning to Madrid, with the prospect of a job on the horizon; an 'Auxiliar de Conversacion.' A bit like the Camino, this was something that I have never heard of or even thought about doing before. I went to the school on the 9th January. I was all smartly dressed, had my C.V in my hand ready for the interview, only to arrive and was welcomed with open arms by the head teacher. She gave me a hug and then the standard cheek-to-cheek Spanish style kisses. She then, showed me around the school and gave me a timetable and said, 'your usual day off is on a Monday, but seeing as you are here, do you want to stay today and have Friday off instead?' To show willing and because I was excited to get stuck in straight away, I said, 'Yes!'

I was very lucky to get the job and it was such a great experience. Both the teachers and children were very friendly, kind and great to work with. Working there was an amazing experience and it was a refreshing break from all the overtime I'd worked in catering.

Madrid is a really lovely city to live in. Firstly the weather is hotter than it is in England and obviously it rains a lot less, then there is the food; paella on a Sunday afternoon; tortilla and warm, fresh bread for breakfast. Also because, there are greengrocers selling fresh fruit and veg all over the city. Seeing so many of those shops actually encouraged me to eat more and eat healthier than I do at home.

The sights of the city are also beautiful. The Royal Palace and Cathedral de Almudena, are two places I'd recommend. The park and grounds around the palace are very relaxing to sit, people watch and catch some sun and the insides of the Cathedral are beautiful, massive stained glass windows and if you are lucky, choir boys singing. Then there are the cosmopolitan streets of Malasaña, where people stand and drink in the streets, rather than being in a bar. I had a few nights, chatting to random people over a few beers in the street. There are guys that walk around with a cool box selling cans of lager for next to nothing.

My favourite place of all though is Parque de Retiro, or to you, and me it'd be known as; Retiro Park. It's a very big park, with pristine pathways, a beautiful glasshouse to see and a huge boating lake. One night, there was a musical fireworks display, which was incredible to watch. It was very similar to the incredible show that was put on, one night in Plaza de Mayor. There were all these laser lights whizzing around in time with the music. The Spanish certainly know how to do things in style, especially when it comes to eating, drinking and partying.

Another thing I liked a lot was the public transport system. It is a lot better, faster, more efficient and cleaner than it is in London. There were no greasy feeling handrails. However, there are the same people who run to catch a train and when they miss it, they try to look very cool and act as if it was unintentional. I have often thought about this and never understood why people do it, particularly as there's always another train that comes along shortly after.

One Friday morning, I almost became one of these people. I was told that I was going on a school trip and I couldn't be late. I got to the station early, bought my routine morning coffee, which took a bit longer than usual to make. I was almost too late and had to run to get the train. I just made it and got on while the loud doors closing noise was going off. As I was trying to squeeze myself onto the train, the doors were closing on my bag and bashed my elbow. It hurt a little and I shouted, 'whoopsie daisies and ouch..' It must have been quite loud too because there were a few laughs, smiles and people staring at me. After I had composed myself, I realised the reason why people were smiling and laughing at me. It wasn't just because of my choice of words, but also because, I had also spilt most of the coffee all down my front!

Camino de Portugués – Oporto to Tui (115k)

As if one Camino wasn't enough. Craig and Mick had decided that we should arrange a reunion. The plan was to meet up in Easter and walk the Camino from Oporto to Santiago de Compostela. It was a great plan and a good idea to get back out on the road again. Unfortunately, I could only get a week off school and walk with them for six days.

During that week, we reminisced about our August adventures and unsurprisingly had a lot to drink, again! On our way walking into one of the towns I said to Craig, 'I bet we end up back here later and drink a lot of bottles of wine.' We then did the usual routine; find an albergue; getting settled in; showered and changed etc. Then it was time for dinner. When we left the albergue; Craig, Mick and I let the girls decide where we were going. Ironically they just happened to pick the same bar that I had talked about and even without my instigating it; we drank, ten bottles of wine. Wow, my head was sore the next day!

I hadn't smoked for over two months and had gone to the gym regularly before we met, so I was a lot fitter and able to walk a lot faster. I walked ahead on my own and spent most of that time thinking about some of the similar things I'd thought of during the Frances Camino; my love life; making friends; feeling lonely. I also thought about my own death again and how I wanted the church to be full for me when that dreadful time comes. What managed to distract me from all these sad thoughts was another injury though! On day one, I had a wee bit too much to drink and fell off a step and had sprained my ankle. So I was hobbling a lot and doing my slap and swallow technique every day and stop. I still managed to walk 120 kilometres though!

The six days walk, went far too quickly. It was a brilliant week and it was lovely to see all the guys again. We all got on so well; it was like we hadn't left each other. I can't wait until the next time we all go out together! During the walk, I confirmed a lot of my previous Camino feelings that despite how difficult things in Madrid were, I was a certainly a happier person and in a better place than I was.

While I whizzed away from them on a train, it felt like I was cheating because I wasn't walking. I got chatting to two lovely girls from Germany, Marie and Lisa. They were great company and made the journey a lot less emotional than it would have been if I were alone. We had a good laugh together on the train. I had even forgotten about the walking too, at least until, there was a shooting pain that went up my leg and brought me back to reality. When we arrived in Santiago, the girls and I, exchanged numbers and made a plan to meet up later that evening for a drink and some dinner together.

I had already booked a place to stay, so I said goodbye to them at the station and I hobbled off to find the albergue. After I'd sorted myself out, the owner of the place, offered to give me a lift into the city. I decided to go for a walk to the small square where the Cathedral entrance is and have a beer to celebrate having arrived. I also thought it might be a good idea to rest my ankle for a bit. It felt quite odd being there again. It was strange not having completed a full Camino journey, watching all the other pilgrims staggering in made me reminisce about my journey. I was thinking about old friends and new friends, Marie and Lisa popped into my mind and I was looking forward to meeting up with them. When suddenly, I received a message from Marie, who suggested that we meet for a drink at 6 p.m., by the Cathedral entrance. Which was perfect for me because it was just after 5 p.m., and I was sat right next to it.

I finished my beer and decided to walk around to the main square. As soon as I turned a corner and saw the square, I felt this overwhelming mix of emotions. I saw the spot where I was sat all those months before and I cried my eyes out. I didn't know what to do with myself. Until, I turned around and right, in front of me was the two girls; Marie and Lisa. I felt like a bit of a wimp, crying in front of two girls, who I'd only just met. Marie, was very sweet; she came over and gave me a hug, which instantly made me feel all right with the world and myself again.

After I'd calmed down and said hello properly, we went to have a look around the Cathedral. Lisa went off on her own and Marie and I looked around together. Within seconds of walking around, I burst into tears again. I was just so overwhelmed by the thought of walking all these pathways and ending up in the Cathedral. Bless Marie was there straight away, with that wonderful healing effect that seems to work for me every time: with another hug and a cuddle. Thank you! That night, we had a lot to drink, played cards and met a lovely Australian couple. It was a great night and was the perfect ending to another Camino. One day, I hope to go there again and walk from the beginning to end in one go!

My end point of the Camino de Portugues

Camino and Madrid life Reflection

When I left London over a year ago, I could have described myself using the following words;

Depressed, sad, bored, tired, in fact, exhausted. I felt really lonely too. I was working so much that I just didn't have the time or energy to make friends and I didn't know how either. I generally just felt negative all over.

When the idea of walking the Camino was planted like a seed in my head. I wanted to go and I am very pleased that it grew big enough, to generate the desire and will to go and do it. Now looking back at all those amazing things happened, I feel very different to all those feelings I had before. My mind feels a lot more serene and happier and my heart feels almost whole again. There were some real miracles I think that happened to me and I am incredibly fortunate and grateful that I was able to be there, witness them and have things change.

Even when I think about this, deep down inside me, on my day one of walking the Camino Frances. I didn't know why I was going, other than my friend having given me the idea. I needed to escape my depressing life and see some different scenery. But the more I walked and the more I thought about everything. I soon realised that what I was actually walking for, was for me to finally deal with the loss of losing my dad and recover from my fear of having any more epilepsy fits. I also gradually started to feel more comfortable being on my own and more confident that my dad would be proud of me.

Arriving and leaving the Cruz de Hierro was and still is, one of the most significant memories that I have from that journey. Feeling like the air was blowing through me and that the pressure, which was on my shoulders was drifting away, was very strange and I really cannot explain it. Despite my midriff, still being a bit too big and wobbly around the edges, somehow, I now feel lighter.

Deciding to walk more Camino's has been good for me and I don't think that I will stop, because of how good it feels before, during and after. Craig, the others and I came up with the term, 'The Camino God.' Who I think, is the person largely responsible for all the miraculous changes that have happened in my life. I no longer feel any of those negative feelings that I had before. Walking over 1000 kilometres, reflecting on everything that has happened to me so far, I feel very fortunate that I have been able to walk all that way and find a new strength within me.

After hearing other peoples' reasons, of why they are walking a Camino, I have realised that my life stories are nowhere near as bad as other people have experienced. Which has made me feel very humble and even more grateful that my yellow arrow road has led me to where I am today.

During my Frances and Portugues, Camino adventures, I have suffered from a lot of injuries; tendinitis in both shins; some horrific blisters. The open wounds on my feet as a result of being an idiot trying to deal with blisters. Then the worst of all, spraining my ankle when being drunk, walking over 120 kilometres and having to take two weeks off school to rest. This was all pretty bad luck, but strangely made both of these Camino's more memorable. It was hilarious being given the name Captain Hoppalong by the guys during both of these journeys and it certainly seemed quite appropriate, given my inability to walk without a slight limp.

Since starting my third Camino, so far there has been no hobbling or injuries. More than likely, this is because I haven't been doing it all in one go. But I am thinking to myself, who knows what might happen this time. Having suffered from a lot of pain and accidents so far, it would be nice for something else to happen. Perhaps the rule; 'third time lucky' might come true and I won't have any injuries. What would be nice would be to make even more friends and maybe even find a nice girl that could become;
Mrs Hoppalong.

Deciding to change my life by leaving London, with the uncertainty of what would happen to me, walking a very long way, staying in an unknown city and working as a teacher. Has been the greatest experience ever and is one of the fundamental reasons, why I wanted to share this story.

When I returned to Madrid after the Portuguese trip. I decided it would be a good time to sort out the loneliness side of life. Which I can see now after writing this book, it seems that being alone is something that has troubled me for a long time.

I have always spent my time working too much to make any real friends, least of all meet a nice girl and be in a relationship. During the Camino's I had the time and the energy and met some really lovely people, all of whom are now very dear and special friends and my ways wouldn't have been quite so special without them.

But, loneliness is sadly, something that has always bothered me a lot. For some reason, not a lot of people like to talk about it either? I don't see it like that because we all have a stage in our life where we must feel like this? At least I like to think so. For me, during these walks, I clearly thought about it a lot, partly because of my fear of having an epileptic fit and there not being anyone to help me, but I think it's mainly because I want to share my experiences with people because of my sociable and friendly character.

One day, when I was thinking about this, I came up with this acrostic poem, which now seems quite appropriate for me in my life.

Lonely

Lonely is an
Old feeling for me, for
Now and
Every day since
Loneliness was only in my life until last
Year

Anyway, after the Portuguese Camino, I decided that I didn't want to rely on my Madrid friend anymore and it was time to make some friends of my own. My idea was to join some groups on Facebook and see where that got me. One afternoon a few days after getting back from Portugal, I was browsing through the group's section and seeing which ones I could join. I had to think for a while, what my interests are because I'd never had a chance to have any. Eventually, I settled for a hiking group, requested to join and thought let's see what happens.

A few days later, I was accepted and saw that there were some people going out for a hike that weekend. I asked the girl in charge of the group if I could go and she said yes, if I wanted to all I had to do was give her my phone number. An hour later, she had added me into a Whatsapp chat with over 40 people in it, who were all discussing the arrangements for the hike. I remember seeing some ridiculous questions. 'Won't it be too hot at 11 a.m., to walk?' 'Do I need to bring a torch?' 'Do I need a sleeping bag?'

There were more questions throughout the week too. 'Should I bring a tent and cooking stove in case it rains?' Bear in mind this was in April and we were in Spain? It was only a day trip walking for a few hours in a national park. It frustrated me, reading such nonsense, so I asked the woman that had added me in if I could organise it. She said, 'yes.' So I did, I met 15 people, had a great explore around a beautiful mountain place called La Pedriza. There is a beautiful stream, river and some lovely rocks to climb up and over. It's a great place to go hiking. Part of the Camino even goes through there too.

After going out on this trip, I decided that I would set up a group of my own and post events and things that I wanted to do in a month and invite people.

I called the group, 'Madventures,' partly because of my name, as in 'Matt's adventures.' But I also realised that the adventures could be mad, crazy good kind or even 'Madrid adventures.' Anyway, at one point, there were over two hundred people who had joined, and I had only started it with the four people I knew in Madrid.

From April to July, I organised a lot of different events, based upon things I saw in a magazine or heard from others. It was a great experience because I met a group of people who turned out to be the loveliest and greatest bunch to spend time with. We went out on a lot of trips together, for example; a visit to the Monastery in El Escorial, to a palace in a place called Aranjuez. I organised a few curry dinners and trips out and about. One of the girls I became friends with, even hosted a Karaoke night, which was great fun. One of the best guys I'd met, loved to play cards even more than me, so we passed a lot of time, playing 'Shit Head' and drinking a lot of red wine; mainly because at 2.50€ a bottle, why not.

So it turned out that I'd made a good bunch of friends and had people to hang out with, which was a good feeling. What bothered me though, was why there were so many other people in the group that didn't want to join in. For example, one afternoon, I asked the group, 'does anyone want to do something this weekend?' Which it seems to me like it's a simple question? I posted this on a Tuesday, by Thursday had been seen by over one hundred people, and only five people replied. All of which were the friends that I already knew. Perhaps it says something about me or maybe they were just busy. But what bothered me the most is that it only takes seconds to write a reply.

Forming the group was a good idea, because it made me realise that my main driving force to make friends was because of that idea of having a full church for my funeral.

Recently I have come to the conclusion that I am no longer bothered about being on my alone, because I would rather have just one friend and they be the best in the world, than have a church full of people who don't know the real me and how much of a special friend I can be. I saw this quote, which is part of the Sermon on the Mount and presents what is known as the golden rule;

'Therefore whatever you desire for men to do to you, you shall also do to them; for this is the law and the prophets.'
The World English Bible, Matthew, 7:12

One other important thing that seems to have come out of writing this is this idea of making other people proud, namely my dad. To fully understand the meaning of the word, I asked some friends what their first thoughts were when I said to them, 'Proud.'

The funniest answer I was given was;
"When I think of pride, I think of France."

Another friend gave me a long-winded explanation about Pride, being proud, etc. But then settled on the word; Aspiration. Which according to the Oxford dictionary is;

'A hope or ambition of achieving something.'

Well, I have certainly achieved something. I have walked a very long way and thought a lot about my family and myself. Which, has given me hope, that my life can be better and I can be happier. This has made me think, how special I am as a person has boosted my confidence, love and appreciation of myself. It also made me realise, that I am enough and should not dwell on the negativity and the fears and sadness that was once all my life was about.

While I am still trying to make my Dad and family proud. What I think is more important now, is that I should be proud of myself. I am the one who is in control of my destiny. It is possible to be influenced by others, but the free will and final decision-making comes from within me.

If it weren't for Rachel and that guy, I wouldn't have heard of the Camino, but if it weren't for my ability to make that difficult first step and go, none of what has happened would be true. After all of the pain, fear and loneliness that I have felt. Having walked all these 'ways,' I am very lucky that I have become a very different and more positive person, living a very different and happier life.

Achieving all these walks and writing this book, has taken a lot of time, effort and determination, which for the first time in my life has made me think, 'Matt.. You should be proud of yourself!'

My family have also said it to me, but unfortunately that doesn't feel as inspiring as it does for me to have knowing that no matter what I do, my dad will always be proud of me!

I have even had friends say it to me too. Out of the blue, I received a message from a friend I lived with ten years ago. She said to me;

'I love seeing your photos on here chicken, you look so happy and I am so pleased you left London, I am very proud of you.'

When I told my told Mum and Craig that I had written this book. They both had the same first reaction; 'Wow, do you feel any different?'

The only answer I can say is; I felt different the moment I walked out of our front door and have been happier every day since.

Writing this has been a great experience for me and I hope that you have enjoyed reading it and maybe feel inspired to take on the challenge of walking a Camino or even take the first difficult step and make some changes in your life. I have definitely learnt that the hardest part of any change is taking that first step and hoping for the best!

The statement, 'I am who I am because of everyone' is how I started my literary journey and it is also how I would like it to end. I would not be half the man I was, had I not grown up in such a wonderful family, met some exceptionally kind people during my Camino 'ways' and having lived through some amazing and miraculous experiences, which I hope will continue!

All the photos included in this book are of memorable people, places and moments. My favourite one is directly underneath one of my favourite words; The Camino stone and LOVE.

It's such a simple word to say and easy to write, but a lot better to think and feel, without love, we are nothing but empty, sad, unhappy and depressed, which is not a good way to live!

Truly, 'I am who I am' because of the love that I had from my wonderful dad and have from all of my family and some friends too.

Just before I was leaving Madrid, another random thing happened. I decided by chance to go to the Plaza de Santiago and church on the 25th July (the very day I left London.) Only to be reminded that it is Santiago the Apostle's day. So I stayed and saw an incredible service.

With love, hugs and gratitude to you all.

Captain H / Matt

Buen Camino = Buen Life.

Oh and if you fancy a walk with me one day, feel free to get in touch; captainhoppalong@gmail.com

25th July 2016. Plaza de Santiago and Church
Santiago the Apostol going walkabout
The St. James' day mass

What's next?

Well having finished writing this book, it seems quite right to say that I am a very different person. Particularly, regarding my outlook on things, my thoughts on loneliness, pride and all of the negative feelings that I'd once had are not the same. I am certainly happier and much more content.

In terms of my career, well.. because I had a great time working at the primary school and a summer camp, I worked at in July. I decided to come home to London and go to university to study a PGCE in a primary school and specialise in Spanish. I had applied for a loan, chosen three universities and had everything all sorted before I moved back to the U.K and into my parent's house again. Which has been great because it's nice to see all my family and have a comfortable bed and an amazing bathroom again. But anyway, the first two universities rejected me, because I haven't worked in a school in England but was lucky once again and I was offered a place from my third choice. It was a very exciting feeling, knowing that I was going to be able to become a 'proper' teacher.

The British Department for Education stipulates that any person wishing to undergo any teacher training, must pass a numeracy and literacy test before undertaking any studying. I duly booked these tests and failed them both. I hastily booked them for a week later, passed the Literacy, but failed the Numeracy. So, rather than rushing and wasting my third and final attempt at doing the maths, I studied for 5-6 hours per day, for two weeks and failed again! I had improved though.

I failed each test by, 7 then 5 and then 2 marks. Sadly, because of these strict requirements, I've had to wave goodbye to this route of teaching and have spent the last two weeks, searching my soul and exploring what I want to do next. So far, I haven't come up with any major answers.. But let's see; I'm sure the 'Camino God' is out there watching and looking after me. There's a reason why I didn't go to university and perhaps, now I've finished focusing all my energy writing, fate will guide me and explain the answer.

From the right; Orla, Craig, Jane, Myself, Emily & Mick

From the right; Myself, Tosha, Colin, Mick, Craig & Orla

107

Lisa, Marie and I, in Santiago de Compostela

Having a little lie down for a minute

To us, who lost ourselves
in the process of loving
someone and forgot that
we are special too.
Buen Camino! May
We ~~....~~ regain our
Self-love and realize
We are enough !!!

My credencial books complete with stamps
& my walking sticks

Dad..
I am and will always be
forever grateful to you and mum for
all that you did and still do....

I love you both, so very much!

Celebrating my 18th Birthday with my mum & dad

Printed in Great Britain
by Amazon